Making Sense of Work Through Collaborative Storytelling

Tricia Cleland Silva
Paulo de Tarso Fonseca Silva

Making Sense of Work Through Collaborative Storytelling

Building Narratives in Organisational Change

palgrave
macmillan

Tricia Cleland Silva
Department of Management and Organization
Hanken School of Economics
Helsinki, Finland

Paulo de Tarso Fonseca Silva
Metaphora International
Helsinki, Finland

ISBN 978-3-030-89445-0 ISBN 978-3-030-89446-7 (eBook)
https://doi.org/10.1007/978-3-030-89446-7

This Palgrave Macmillan imprint is published by the registered company Springer Nature Switzerland AG.
The registered company address is: Gewerbestrasse 11, 6330 Cham, Switzerland

In loving memory of Dona Josefa,
Mother, Grandmother, Teacher
1932–2019

Preface

Working with stories is about being curious and interested. It is about engaging with people who have lived embodied experiences without making assumptions or providing advice. It is about holding space and actively listening to someone else making sense of their own identity and position through empathy not sympathy.

Empathy is different from sympathy. Empathy is the ability to understand and share the feelings of another, without taking responsibility for those feelings through advice or actions. Empathy is about sitting and being present to hear someone making sense of their experiences without judgement or expectation.

To tell one's story authentically is truth telling. It is truth telling as it can give consent to the reality of what is within a particular time, place, and culture from the perspective of one's experiences. When the storyteller is not fully listened to, there is a risk of giving shallow meaning to the story based on one's own limitations. This risk can lead to destructive material consequences by restricting people to a story that they did not choose. This risk affects all of us, but it is more common for individuals who do not belong to the dominant social group.

Usually, when we explain lived experiences through stories, we draw from metaphors to give imagery to our present thinking, recollection of the past, and hopes for the future. Like getting better at a craft, storytelling allows us to discover patterns of what works and what could be reinvented in the stories and metaphors we tell to others with a meaningful purpose. Our stories are embodied, and we carry them with us no matter where we are, influencing each experience.

Stories are powerful and can dictate how one behaves and sees oneself in their work role as well as in asserting one's identity. The power of stories draws attention to the reality that we do not check our embodied stories at the door when we enter the workplace. We are our stories, but often, the stories that we embody remain uninvited or under acknowledged at the workplace.

Ignoring stories does not make them go away but rather creates obstacles to collaboration and engagement with each other and the work itself.

Acknowledging stories means acknowledging emotions. Emotions are evoked during organisational change, so it is fair to say that stories and metaphors are also evoked whether we are conscious of them or not. When stories are restricted at work, especially during times of uncertainty, fear festers and suppresses creativity, trust, and the motivation to collaborate for the intended organisational change. The amount of sense given to the change by those in positions of power does not matter. If the stories and metaphors do not align with the meaning given by those affected by the change, collaboration will be tainted by confusion, mistrust, and disengagement.

This book is about how we mediate stories at the workplace during times of organisational change. Stories with a work as craft mindset can help others to make sense of their working roles, tools, resources, and the purpose of a community of practice through Collaborative Storytelling.

Throughout the book, we discuss our values and beliefs as Story Mediators and for Collaborative Storytelling with our method of Collaborative Story Craft. The book aims to provide a theoretical framework and tools, including potential practices to build trust and collaboration with those who are challenged to make sense of an activity during times of change.

This book is the outcome of a collaborative process with a deep meaningful purpose of working with stories to empower inclusive and consensual change, which acknowledges and draws from all the stories affected. Within our work practice, we see our roles as Story Mediators. Embodying our values and beliefs at work and in our social worlds, we are also Story Craftivists. As Story Craftivists, our mission is to empower authentic stories and help people work better together.

Helsinki, Finland

Tricia Cleland Silva
Paulo de Tarso Fonseca Silva

Acknowledgments

We would like to acknowledge the Academy of Finland and Hanken School of Economics for funding and supporting Tricia's work through the writing of this book and making it Open Access. A special thanks also to Jess Kelley (The Write Kelley) for keeping us accountable to each other and ourselves during the collaborative processes of writing.

Contents

About the Authors

Tricia Cleland Silva and Paulo de Tarso Fonseca Silva are a multicultural family who live and work in Helsinki, Finland. Tricia holds a PhD in Management and Organisation from Hanken School of Economics, and Paulo de Tarso holds a Masters in Adult Education from the Center for Research on Activity, Development and Learning (CRADLE), University of Helsinki.This book is based on their work as *Story Mediators* with their method of *Collaborative Story Craft*. Their method is used in their practices through their consultancy business Metaphora International, their teaching and research within universities, and other communities of practice. The theory of *Collaborative Storytelling* is a deeper reflection of their work, and it embodies their values and beliefs as a couple, parents, and members of many social worlds.

Abbreviations

CL	Change Laboratory
CHAT	Cultural-Historical Activity Theory
CSA	Collaborative Storytelling Activity
CSAS	Collaborative Storytelling Activity System
CSC	Collaborative Story Craft
TILES	Trade, Inclusion, Liberty, Equilibrium, and Sustainability

List of Figures

CHAPTER 1

Introduction

Abstract Collaborative Storytelling is a theory of social and cultural change. The theory itself advocates for space and time to reflect on social identities and embodied lived experiences through stories. In this chapter, we introduce how metaphors, narratives and stories powerfully impact organisational change in exclusive or inclusive ways.

Keywords Communities of practice • Emotional tax • Exclusion • Metaphorical stories • Organisational change

Until you make the unconscious conscious, it will direct your life and you will call it fate
—Carl Jung

This book is about building inclusive narratives in organisational change by making sense of work through *Collaborative Storytelling*. Collaborative Storytelling is a theory of social and cultural change which advocates for space and time to reflect on social identities and embodied, lived experiences through stories in relation to an activity. Like in all social settings, everyone at the workplace is a storyteller, and their stories can inform and

T. Cleland Silva, P. de Tarso Fonseca Silva, *Making Sense of Work Through Collaborative Storytelling*,
https://doi.org/10.1007/978-3-030-89446-7_1

reveal common themes that can unite actors towards intentional and committed change.

Organisational change is cultural change as it questions assumptions, values, and beliefs that underlie current realities (Alvesson and Sveningsson 2015). Storytelling can reveal meaning and intentions of organisational members, the work, and the purpose of the change without committing the error of acting on it without consent (Cleland Silva and Fonseca Silva 2021).

Metaphors and stories are strong communication channels to emotions and embodied lived experiences, especially in times of uncertainty and vulnerability (Broussine and Vince 1996, p. 6). Exploring and opening up the metaphors and stories can initiate a conversation as to what is actually going on, without isolating or marginalising individuals' perceptions. People need to believe in the benefit of the change, and that their contribution is supported, acknowledged, and purposeful.

Individual and collective conflicts arise when dominant narratives (including metaphors and stories) are imposed on individuals without meaningful discussion or consent. Exclusive narratives have the potential to block creativity, motivation, and prevent individuals from engaging with purposeful and rewarding work. A single dominant story is dangerous and risks critical misunderstandings of another person's assumptions and lived experiences (Ngozi Adichie 2009).

At work, individuals bring their own stories and lived experiences to a community of practice.

> Communities of Practice (CoPs) are groups of people brought together through an activity system or "practice" (Lave and Wenger 1991) within a cultural-historical context. Members of the CoPs are connected by what they do and their abilities to practice with certain tools and defined objectives, roles, and rules. A CoP can develop naturally, as the members' common interests motivate them to share their knowledge and experiences through storytelling.

Through the exchange of stories about the activity, each member of a community has an opportunity to learn from each other. At the same time, each member from different social worlds brings unique stories that are embodied and relational, based on their lived experiences. For instance, a teacher, born and raised in a city by immigrant parents, working at a rural elementary school, shares stories from a social position that is different from their colleague who was educated and raised in the same area of the school. Even though both teachers have the same university degree, access to similar school resources, and their work has similar rules and objectives, their engagement at work, relationships, and performance are influenced by how they perceive themselves and how others perceive them.

Most often, when stories are exchanged, they are filled with metaphors as metaphors can invoke or activate stories (Snaevarr 2010, p. 233).

Metaphor, as a word, originates from Greek 'amphora', a storage container used to transport valuable goods. This definition is a metaphor in itself as metaphors are figures of speech to describe, experience, and understand "one kind of thing in terms of another" (Lakoff and Johnson 2003, p. 5) or transport "meaning" from one kind of thing to another. Metaphors have the power to not only transfer meaning, but also provoke, transform, and bridge interpretations of the world, including the stories we tell and are told.

In various ways, metaphors can support sensemaking, not only our physical reality but also our inner imaginary landscape. Metaphors can transform stories through narration and their interpretation may evolve, especially in group conversations. When this happens, an opportunity arises to collaborate and create a *metaphorical story* (Gibbs 2013) that resonates (or conflicts) with the members of the group. In communities of practice, a metaphorical story can engage members in collective sensemaking aligned with the purpose of the work activity, affording new opportunities for change (Cleland Silva and Fonseca Silva 2019).

As stories and metaphors carry dominant patterns of narratives in an activity and/or narrative systems, individuals may not feel psychologically or physically safe to exchange stories with others, mainly with those who hold more powerful positions in terms of authority at work or social privilege. This is especially true when the dominant stories or metaphors conflict with individual lived experiences and personal values and beliefs. These conflicts can be harmful for the individual and manifest in physical and psychological ways, which the NGO, Catalyst, in a 2018 report, calls "emotional tax."

"Emotional tax" is an effect of workplace exclusion on emotions, mind, and body based on biases of the employees' social identity such as gender, race, and/or ethnicity. In the 2018 report from the NGO Catalyst, employees shared how these impacted (or taxed) their physical and psychological health in painful and unhealthy ways (Dnika and Thorpe-Moscon 2018, p. 4). For example, Ty, a 27 year old White and Latino man, describes the bias identified by his hair (2018, p. 6):

> *Before a [job] interview, I changed the appearance of my hair to make it look more like the hair texture/style of the majority of the people at the [company].*

Whereas, Tena, a 25 year old Black Latina, talks about how her identity is constructed through different channels of communication and subsequently her identity is 'suppressed' by her superiors (Dnika and Thorpe-Moscon 2018, p. 6):

> *I work from home, so none of my callers can see me. Based on the sound of my voice they assume I am a young, Caucasian female, and so they are very comfortable making very racist comments against different nationalities. I have to pretend that I am not offended, and I am encouraged by my superiors to suppress my true identity.*

Throughout life, we navigate many social worlds that construct and impact our sense of self.

Social worlds are groups of people who share common beliefs and values, and individuals are committed to these worlds based on their sense of identity, purpose, and contribution (Strauss 1978).

Intersecting social worlds are larger systems of narratives that act as invisible forces, influencing us consciously and unconsciously. Exploring these systems for patterns of meaning through storytelling helps us to reflect and potentially communicate our position in a social world and the way our sense of self impacts and is perceived by others.

Systems of narratives affect social worlds and individuals differently and unequally. Identities constructed and developed in social worlds intersect with individual attributes, such as ethnicity, gender, sexual orientation, class, language, religion, nationality, and physical and mental abilities. Most often, socially constructed identities interwoven in systems of narratives influence access to education, income, employment, health, and even life expectancy (e.g., hooks 2000 on class). In other words, social identities constructed by stories and narratives have material consequences for our physical bodies, our emotions, and our positional status.

People's lives have multiple stories, but the potential of these stories is restricted by powerful systems of narratives (White 2007) and dominant social worlds. To build narratives during organisational change, individuals need to start with their own stories, reflecting on their past and present experiences and their social identity.

From an early age, we have been taught ways of thinking and behaving through spoken and performed stories. Those stories create a sense of self about, which community we belong to, and what our purpose and roles are in that community. Stories have a powerful impact on our surroundings and contribute to larger systems of collective meaning, influencing which stories are accepted, challenged, ignored, or silenced.

Cultivating personal power and a sense of responsibility to others starts with knowing and valuing who you are. In other words, telling your story with self-awareness, challenging narratives that do not represent one's reality, and holding yourself accountable for the stories you tell.

In this book, we narrate metaphorical stories to explain the concepts used in *Collaborative Storytelling* with the tool *Collaborative Story Craft* (CSC). We invite the reader to engage with their inner imaginary landscape through stories and reflect on their own social positioning. The metaphorical stories are narrated from our empirical research, other literary sources, and our own lived experiences.

References

Alvesson, Mats, and Stefan Sveningsson. 2015. *Changing organizational culture: Cultural change work in progress.* 2nd ed. New York: Routledge.

Broussine, Mike, and Russ Vince. 1996. Working with metaphor towards organizational change. *Organisation development: Metaphorical explorations*, 57.

Cleland Silva, Tricia, and Paulo de Tarson Fonseca Silva. 2019. Validating change through collaborative story craft. *SAGE Research Methods Cases Part 2 (SAGE*

Research Methods Cases). Thousand Oaks: SAGE. https://doi.org/10.4135/9781526478245.

Cleland Silva, Tricia, and Paulo de Tarso Fonseca Silva. 2021. Collaborative story craft as a tool for inclusive workplace practices. In *History and business storytelling*, ed. Albert Mills, Nick Deal, and David Boje. Singapore: World Scientific.

Dnika, Travis J., and Jennifer Thorpe-Moscon. 2018. *Day-to-Day experiences of emotional tax among women and men of color in the workplace*. Toronto: Catalyst. https://www.catalyst.org/wp-content/uploads/2019/02/emotionaltax.pdf.

Gibbs, Raymond W., Jr. 2013. Walking the walk while thinking about the talk: Embodied interpretation of metaphorical narratives. *Journal of Psycholinguistic Research* 42 (4): 363–378.

hooks, bell. 2000. *Where we stand: Class matters*. New York: Routledge.

Lakoff, George, and Mark Johnson. 2003. *Metaphors we live by*. Chicago: The University of Chicago Press. (Original work published 1980).

Lave, Jean, and Etienne Wenger. 1991. *Situated learning: Legitimate peripheral participation*. Cambridge: Cambridge University Press.

Ngozi Adichie, Chimamanda. 2009. The danger of a single story. *Ted Talk Global*, October 7. https://www.ted.com/talks/chimamanda_ngozi_adichie_the_danger_of_a_single_story.

Snævarr, Stefán. 2010. *Metaphors, narratives, emotions: Their interplay and impact*. Leiden: Brill.

Strauss, Anselm L. 1978. Social worlds perspective. *Studies in Symbolic Interaction* 1, ed. Norman Denzin: 119–128.

White, Michael. 2007. *Maps of narrative practice*. New York: W. W. Norton.

CHAPTER 2

Making Sense of Work through Collaborative Storytelling

Abstract Similar to social identities, each story and its narration is unique and yet relational and situated in a context of history, culture, and materiality. In this chapter, we explore local and global systems of narratives and their powerful influence on the stories and metaphors we tell and we are told to make sense of our embodied lived experiences. Through our theory of *Collaborative Storytelling*, we discuss how *Collaborative Storytelling Activity*, with the tool *Collaborative Story Craft*, expands individual and collective sensemaking at work to build inclusive narratives in organisational change.

Keywords Communities of practice • Embodiment • Metaphors • Narratives • Power • Sensemaking • Social and cultural scripts • Stories • Storytelling

When the storyteller tells the truth, she reminds us that human beings are more alike than unalike.
—Maya Angelou

Each individual possesses unique stories based on their social identities, relationships, and embodied experiences in a material world. Our bodies and social material worlds are based on interacting systems that have

T. Cleland Silva, P. de Tarso Fonseca Silva, *Making Sense of Work Through Collaborative Storytelling*,
https://doi.org/10.1007/978-3-030-89446-7_2

purpose, roles, and practices which influence and regulate our choices, how we act, our daily routines, our relationships, our work life, and local and global governance. Each individual is uniquely impacted by these systems in different ways that range from empowering to oppressive.

Intersecting these systems are powerful narratives that affect how stories are signified and told (Snævarr 2010, p. 168).

> Narrative is defined as a sequence of events with a beginning, series of unfolding events but not necessarily an ending (Halverson et al. 2011, p. 11).

Narratives are produced and accessible to others through different means such as written texts, spoken words, pictures, symbols, artefacts, and so forth (Cleland Silva and Fonseca Silva 2019, p. 86). A narrative requires both a narrator and an audience, whose viewpoints and social identities affect how the narrative is received (Gabriel 2004). For instance, a narration sent through a work email about an event is received differently than a conversation in the coffee room about the same or similar event.

In this way, narrative is not simply reporting what has been done but rather how the individuals feel about the story they are telling (Greenhalgh 1999). While being narrated, the story provides agency to the narrator as the story "can float freely for any talk about a sequence of events" (Labov 2013, p. 18).

> A story is what is being recounted which differs from the way the story is told through narration. In this respect, narratives can be understood as signifiers, whereas stories can be seen as the signified (Snævarr 2010, p. 168). This said, stories do not have to be restrained by narratives, and yet, the narrator or receiver may believe that stories are.

In local and global systems, certain stories can dominate or be restrained by narratives (White 1995) which are based on the individual's social position and identity as well the individual's perception of self in relation to others. For instance, based on the cultural and historical context, narratives can construct stories of the "ideal worker" (see Acker 1990, 2006), the "good immigrant" (Shukla 2016), or the "caring nurse" (Cleland Silva 2019), which have material consequences for the actors affected by the narration. Material consequences can be, for instance, the "ideal worker" receiving higher pay than the "caring nurse," whose work is constructed as a "calling" rather than of productive value. This highlights power relations in stories based on social identities which are embedded in the local and global systems of narratives.

Exclusive Narratives

Exclusive narratives that construct stories of others come with a cost (Cleland Silva and Fonseca Silva 2021). For instance, narratives in the workplace that are imposed on the employees can lead to confusion, disengagement, and isolation. The challenges of identifying oneself in the collective story limit the opportunities of organisational growth and sustainable ways to collaborate.

These unconscious biases can mindlessly be incorporated in the organisation's culture, creating work practices based on stereotype narratives. As exemplified by Ng and Sears's article "Walking the talk on diversity" (2020), narratives of managers and leaders send messages to the employees of how the organisation constructs diversity and practices of inclusion. If the narratives are exclusive, the practices will continue to exclude employees with detrimental effects on the individual well-being, motivation, and organisational performance.

When the workplace prevents individual narratives and identities to be represented in a common story and practices, the culture of the organisation enables a narrow sense of lived experiences. Exclusive narratives and practices not only harm the individual but also send a message that the employees' only option, in order to be themselves, is to leave the organisation (Dnika and Thorpe-Moscon 2018, p. 4). Or, if they stay, they feel obliged to "bargain" with the employers' dominant narratives to work with their sense of purpose and skills (Cleland Silva 2019, p. 173). The sensitivity of knowing how to identify and address exclusion and inclusion in the workplace narratives highlights how important it is to talk openly about differences (Dnika et al. 2016).

Confronting or countering narratives that exclude actors, who subsequently feel "on guard" (Dnika and Thorpe-Moscon 2018, p. 4), requires a recentring of the story, shifting the narratives from the dominant "in group" to the peripheral "out group" (Choudhury 2015, pp. 82–84). This is a process that the organisation must support, facilitate, and incorporate into their strategies and workplace activities. Policies of diversity are not enough to create an organisational culture which is inclusive. For social and cultural change to take place, leaders have to acknowledge the stories and narratives that they share, promote, and encourage versus the narratives and stories that they ignore, belittle, and silence.

There is an old Yiddish saying "what is truer than truth? The story." Story can serve as a communication tool in processes of making explicit sense of events (Eshraghi and Taffler 2015) and through metaphorical lenses, the story harnesses the complexity of people's emotional states (Fainsilber and Ortony 1987), especially during change (Smollan 2014). A good story that resonates and connects the narrator with the receiving audience helps to communicate and make sense of our deeper collective lived experiences (Weick 1995, p. 61).

Let us tell you a story about truth that has been told in many languages and cultures. This is our narration.

Truth and Story

There once was an old woman who was tired, hungry, and weary from her travels. She came upon a small village which she entered in search of hospitality, food, and rest.
She knocked on the first house's door, which was soon answered by a young man who glared at the old woman with disgust.
"What do you want?" he asked with impatience.
"Please, I am hungry and thirsty. Would you be so kind to invite me in and offer your hospitality?" requested the old woman.
"Absolutely not! Can't you see I am a busy man? I have no time for you!" he sneered.
On she went and at every door she knocked, she was either turned away, unacknowledged or even screamed at and spat on.
Giving up her search for hospitality, the old woman went to the village's square and sat by a well-kept fountain.
It may have been a few minutes or hours, the old woman could not recall, but when she raised her eyes, she saw a beautiful stranger in a long golden cloak entering the village.

(*continued*)

(continued)

This stranger knocked on the same doors whose residents rejected the old woman. But, this time, the stranger was greeted with a warm reception and an abundance of kindness. She was told over and over again, "Please enter!" and "What a pleasure it is to meet you!"

And, could you believe it? Even laughter could be heard in the air as the stranger skipped her way through the village from door to door.

As the beautiful stranger thanked her last host, she glanced over to the village's square and spotted the old woman, who still sat by the fountain, feeling both weak from her travels and defeated from her poor reception. The beautiful stranger approached the old woman and asked, "Dear woman, why do you look so sad?"

The old woman replied, "After a long journey, I sought food, water, and rest in the same houses that you have entered, but after looking at me, none of the villagers thought I was worth their attention."

Acknowledging her privilege and feeling a strong sense of responsibility, the beautiful stranger replied, "Would you consider coming back to the same houses with me? I have a long cloak that I could embrace you under and at the very least, you will be able to enter the homes."

The old woman agreed, not only because she needed food and water but also that she was charmed and intrigued by the stranger's presence.

As both women walked towards the first house together, the beautiful stranger said, "I still don't know your name."

The old woman replied, "My name is Truth, what is your name?"

The beautiful stranger smiled and answered, "My name is Story."

As the women entered the houses, the villagers saw Truth with different eyes.

Take a moment and ask yourself if this story speaks to you.

- Who were the main characters and how do you describe them?
- How did the story make you think?
- How did the story make you feel?
- Was there a problem or conflict that you identified in the story?
- How was that problem or conflict addressed and by whom?
- Did the story evoke a metaphor that you can identify in your reality?

In this situation, there are no right, or wrong answers like in all stories, but rather an active exchange of collaborative sensemaking. Story invites new interpretations, giving possibilities to consent and reconcile with the reality that our social worlds intersect with various narratives, reflecting the uniqueness of human experience.

The Social Worlds of Snakes and Ladders

Most often, stories are, in part or entirely, filled with metaphors which are used as an entry point to dialogue amongst people to make sense of larger, complex social systems. Metaphors are defined as "the phenomenon whereby we talk and, potentially, think about something in terms of something else" (Semino 2008, p. 1) and stories filled with metaphors are metaphorical stories (Gibbs 2013; Cameron et al. 2010).

According to Marshak (1996), recurring metaphors in organisations create an invisible force that influences our behaviours and ways of thinking. He calls this invisible force a metaphoric field which is "an interrelated set of conscious to unconscious, explicit to tacit, core to peripheral, organizing themes that are expressed metaphorically and which structure perception and behaviour" (Marshak 1996, p. 152). By identifying these themes, Marshak believes that we can inform ourselves about "conscious, pre-conscious and unconscious assumptions, beliefs and patterns" (ibid.), and the ways in which these metaphors impact our behaviour. For instance, Marshak writes that if organisational change efforts are consistent with the metaphoric field, members are able to relate to the change, even if the change is not fully accepted. On the other hand, if the efforts are inconsistent, members "just won't get it" and quickly ignore, disengage, or discard the effort (1993).

Using a metaphorical story to illustrate systems of narratives, we draw from the board game *Snakes and Ladders.*

With Indian origins, the game *Snakes and Ladders* is over a century old, and its original use has its roots in morality lessons: a player's progression up the board reflects life's journey complicated by virtues (ladders) and vices (snakes) (Pritchard 1994, p. 162).
Designed for two players or more, the game is relational. The players are expected to roll a die on their turn, in order to move up the

(*continued*)

(continued)
numbers, through the gridded board. "Ladders" and "snakes" are placed throughout the board, connecting two specific board squares. The object of the game is to navigate the game board, according to the rolls of the dice, from the start (bottom square) to the finish (top square), helped by climbing ladders, but hindered by falling down snakes.

At first glance, the game is a simple race based on sheer luck with a common shared sense of the same reality. However, using the lens of the game's original morality purpose, we can interpret the metaphor of moving up and down ladders as a social system based on narratives of social position, power, and privilege rather than the simplicity of rolling the dice (Fig. 2.1).

Exploring the board game as a system of narratives, we begin to understand power as a social and relational phenomenon (I am winning or I am losing against someone else), but also a psychological one (I lost, therefore, I have bad luck), which we may carry or discard in our own constructed narratives of the world.

If we define power as our capacity to impact or influence our environment (Diamond 2016, p. 3), the game takes on new meaning in terms of where you are positioned on the board (higher or lower number), but also your capacity to influence how you navigate the snakes and the ladders.

Rather than luck, your positioning on the game board applied to real life becomes a sum of your privilege based on your rank in the world, impacting how you navigate and your influence on the larger social system.

Arnold Mindell (1995, 2002), an author, therapist, and teacher in the fields of transpersonal psychology, body psychotherapy, social change, and spirituality, argues that our position and influence in the hierarchy of a social system derives from individual ranks. He describes four sources of these ranks which Julie Diamond (2016, p. 71) divides into social and personal powers in her book *Power: a user guide*.

- Global rank (social power): context dependent, seemingly static and yet based on social norms which are random (e.g., race, wealth/class, religion, gender, sexual orientation, physical ability)
- Local rank (social power): context dependent, changes rapidly and sporadically, associated with local norms, values, conditions, partici-

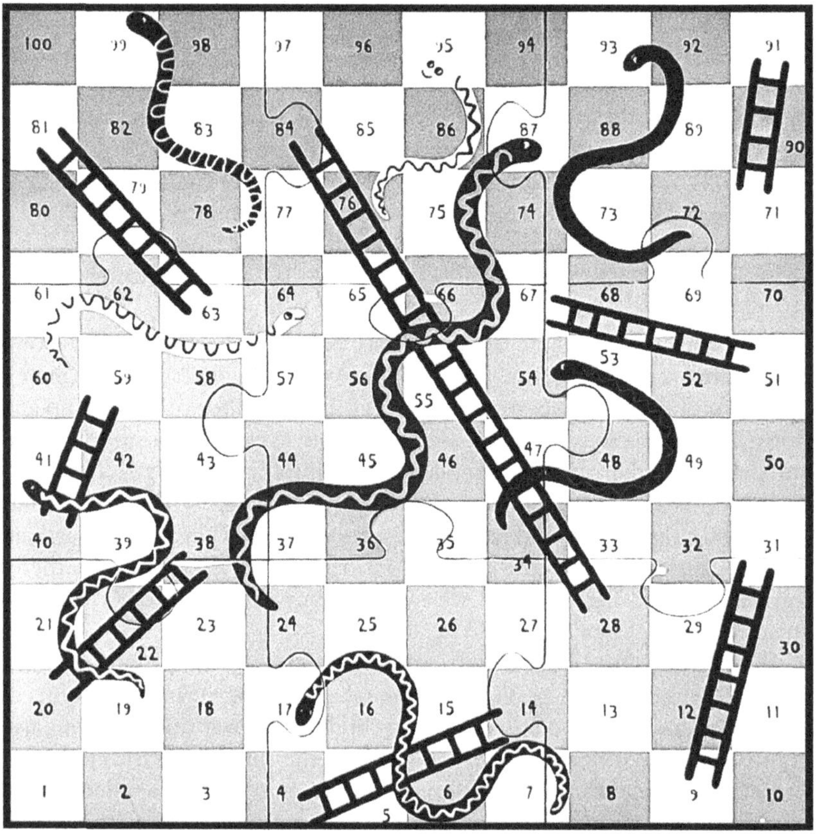

Fig. 2.1 Game of Snakes and Ladders. (Image source: Tricia Cleland Silva, 17.4.21)

pants, topics (e.g., seniority or position in group, compliance to norms, popularity, communication style)

- Psychological rank (personal power): life experiences, emotional fluidity, communication skills, humour, relational skills, insight into self and others
- Spiritual rank (personal power): connection to larger purpose, vision, transcendent experience, knowledge of self and other, awareness of death and life

An individual may navigate their position with ease based on global and local ranks, but their psychological and spiritual rank (or personal power) decides how they socially construct their capacities and courage to deal with the snakes and ladders. In other words, power is both physical as well as a state of mind (Diamond 2016, p. 57).

The ways in which the individual navigates the game board mirrors how social systems of narratives are interpreted, embodied, and emotionally experienced. In parallel to the game and metaphorically speaking, everyone has their own board that represents their lived experiences, revealing the discrepancies of rank in a system of narratives. For instance, the positional rank of individuals on the board is context-specific and may reflect more their position in the dominant social and cultural group rather than luck. In other words, as in the game, the board of these individuals may consist of a privileged discrepancy of ladders versus snakes. Whereas other individuals' boards may limit them to the lower ranks specifically because of the many snakes encountered.

As opposed to the game, where luck is the driving force for action, in practice, having an overview of one's own "board" (and mapping some of the snakes and ladders) can influence choice and decision.

Acknowledging privilege and the position in one's own board also harnesses a sense of the social and personal powers which are occupied in relation to a context. When we can change the context, Viktor Frankl says, "we are challenged to change ourselves" (quoted in Diamond 2016, p. 66). This is personal power, the ability to change ourselves and to get along with even impossible situations, as well as an awareness of responsibility for what the position demands (Diamond 2016, p. 66).

Breaking through the game's metaphor, the possibility of learning from the challenges (snakes) can develop skills on how to deal with further challenges or opportunities by building or even sharing one's own ladder(s).

The "Social Worlds of Snakes and Ladders" metaphorical story is similar to the "multistoried building" metaphor of Michael White, the founder of Narrative Therapy.

White explains that our lives are multi-storied like a building, and institutional practices and systems of narratives restrain individuals to the first floor or one story, which limits the options and possibilities of other stories to help understand a problem.

(*continued*)

(continued)

The main objective of the narrative therapist is to build a "scaffold," a temporary structure outside the building used to support the individual to construct, maintain, and repair their stories. Located on the scaffold, the therapist asks questions to explore the problem and "thin traces" of the stories, which exist through the individual's lived experiences and emerge to build "thickly."[1, 2]

Once the stories are externalised, the individual is empowered to climb the multistories by identifying "unique outcomes" or counter stories to the dominant cultural story or the stories enforced in their social relationships and by institutional practices.

When the individual arrives at the top of their multistoried building, they have a larger perspective of the possibilities to move forward through their own stories and self-mastery of everyday life (White 1995, 2007; Madigan 2011).

Like the explanation of a multistoried building, navigating up the social world of snakes and ladders, individuals move up social rank from small "n" narratives to big "N" narratives.[3] Small "n" narratives are closely located in the person's environment as well as their lived experiences. Small "n" narratives are based on how the person was socialised and developed by their family, community, and institutions in a cultural-historical context. Small "n" narratives are based on the stories that the person is told and has told. Although small, these narratives are potent as they influence how the individual sees their position and navigates the social world.

Big "N" narratives are based on socio-political status. Big "N" narratives accord individuals status based on identity attributes such as race, gender, class, religion, nationality, ethnicity, education, physical and mental ability, and sexual orientation. Big "N" narratives have a huge impact on the opportunities and outcomes we have in life: education, income, employment, health, and life expectancy. For instance, the higher one can climb, the more privileges and advantages one receives in the form of access to resources and information, often bestowing a heightened sense of entitlement to higher positional rank. Hence, the expression "climbing the corporate ladder."

Being high up on the ladder, however, does not always mean that one has a broader perspective on reality. Most often, the higher one climbs, the more isolated the individual becomes from their power's impact on others. This isolation can lead to behaviours that are discriminatory, unequal, and oppressive to others who are lower in the socio-political hierarchy, because they are marginalised or excluded from the big "N" narratives. This not only highlights a deep responsibility for those high up on the ladder and holding people accountable for their use of power, but also a systemic problem that does not critically question the big "N" narratives on the material and social worlds of those excluded.

At the workplace, the Social Worlds of Snakes and Ladders intersect with an activity system based on the community of practice (CoPs). Members of the CoPs internalise shared beliefs, values, and practices based on social interactions while engaging with the object of the work, roles, tools, rules and regulations, and the community. CoP members are assigned roles and tasks both formally and informally. For instance, a member is assigned the role of leader with a designated title and allocated specific tasks and associated material values (e.g., salary) for that position. Informally, the leader may also take on the role of friend and mentor if the leader's values and beliefs align with members of the CoP.

Making sense of work and its social and relational environment is a consensual version of reality, which is an outcome of interpersonal interaction and negotiations (Strauss 1978). Intimately connected to these interactions are individual personal stories, culture, and practices which develop and build relationships. Sensemaking of embodied lived experiences at work, therefore, is about exploring narration of stories as temporal sequences, intentions, meaning, and material outcomes through story sharing. It is also about co-creating new meanings, histories, possibilities, and solutions to the stories that exist among the individual members and in the workplace itself through **Collaborative Storytelling**.

Collaborative Sensemaking of Narratives and Scripts

through life stories individuals and groups make sense of themselves; they tell what they are or what they wish to be, as they tell so they become, they are their stories

—Martin Cortazzi (2001, p. 388)

Sensemaking is an ongoing process by which people give meaning to their individual and collective experiences (Weick et al. 2005, p. 409) through telling a good story (Weick 1995, p. 61). Story is one of the oldest literary forms of understanding cultural heritage and histories of particular times and places to help explain and discern what happened. Story gives plausibility for individual sensemaking of past events that happened in powerful situations influenced by social identities and relationships (Aromaa et al. 2019).

The process of storytelling is a unique embodied experience as the individual uses their senses (sight, touch, hearing, smell, taste) in sensemaking within a social and physical environment (Geertz 1972, p. 86). Social environments, like a workplace, consist of diverse identities which interact, exchange, assert, and negotiate their sense of reality in relation to one another and the activity they are engaging with. As diverse identities coexist, each individual embodies narratives acquired throughout their own lived experiences. Some of these narratives may intersect while others differ, causing tensions and contradictions. As author Anaïs Nin (1961, p. 124) writes, "[w]e do not see things as they are, we see them as we are." This understanding that stories and metaphors hold and carry meaning reveals a profound sense of power and responsibility as to how stories are narrated and spread to larger audiences.

The embodied and highly emotional experience of sensemaking is difficult to communicate and rationalise as it is processed through the uniqueness of the historical context influenced by social and cultural scripts.

> Social scripts are unwritten patterns of human behaviour and ways of acting in response to the social environment, relating the script to the space it exists in and the people who exist in that space (Goffman 1959). Whereas cultural scripts broaden social scripts to patterns of interaction within cultural spaces as these spaces reflect systems of meaning based on grander narratives (Yang et al. 2021).

As described above, in the Social Worlds of Snakes and Ladders, internalised scripts are a driving influence on sensemaking processes. The scripts affect individual behaviours within the situational context, creating and/or reinforcing predominant narratives. While played out and enforced in the workplace context, these predominant narratives are mostly inherited from different historical and cultural social worlds (Bateson 1972).

As big "N" narratives are incorporated into the scripts of the workplace, they tend to "legitimise" certain interactions, including assumptions and expectations as to how people should talk and behave. When left unquestioned, dominant narratives may manifest into practices and policies while problematising or silencing the scripts that do not comply.

With hidden and contradicting scripts, people struggle to make sense of their position in the unfolding story at work, which leads us to the meaning given to **Collaborative Storytelling Activity (CSA).**

Collaborative Storytelling Activity (CSA) is incorporated into a community of practice for revealing and developing the collective meaning afforded to an object of work and understanding a common purpose. CSA draws from the culture and history of the activity through an exchange of stories. CSA in communities is no easy task because it implies **collaborative sensemaking** within the power dynamics of the workplace.

Within the concept of Collaborative Storytelling, we emphasise the action "storytelling" as an on-going craft. In other words, while telling stories, we are also crafting our reality. Therefore, **Collaborative Story Crafting** could be used interchangeably with the same meaning.

We favour Collaborative Storytelling over Collaborative Story Crafting to refer to the activity to make a distinction from the intervention method **Collaborative Story Craft (CSC).**

In Collaborative Storytelling Activity, **Story Mediation** is used to externalise and identify the dominant narratives and scripts that influence common work activities, helping to dismantle and rebuild collective narratives which are based on each member's story. Therefore, the role of a Story Mediator is not originally associated with the community of practice, but rather serves as an external, collaborative support for building narratives in times of change.

Framed as a research activity, the Story Meditator is *with* the storytellers at work.

"Withness thinking" is described by the late John Shotter, an organisational scholar, as a process in which researchers place themselves with those researched (2006, 2010). He asserted that "withness" can only be achieved by conversations between the researcher and the researched through questions and exploring the potentials of the present moment to change possible and future actions (Shotter 2006).

Shotter called this "situated dialogic action research" (Shotter 2006). Whereas other scholars call their methods similar to "withness" as "dialogical mediated inquiry" (Lorino et al. 2011), "collaborative action research" in process theory (Fachin and Langley 2017, p. 320) and "engaged scholarship" (Van de Ven 2007).

Story mediation in our practice with Collaborative Storytelling Activity also implies the use of the intervention method Collaborative Story Craft (CSC). Collaborative Story Craft, as an intervention method, externalises multiple stories based on social relationships and lived experiences. Working with a Story Mediator (through storytelling and crafting), the collaborative effort enables the externalisation of the stories to validate the storyteller's narration at the workplace.

Story Mediation and Collaborative Story Craft

Story Mediation in organisations is an alternative word for intervention, and it is intended to signify a supporting role in a positive process of collaboration with co-creation and applied agency in times of change.

In the workplace, Story Mediation provides a space and an opportunity to reflect on individual stories in relation to the collective work activities. In our practice, Story Mediation was appropriated to fit in the context of a Collaborative Storytelling Activity (CSA) together with the intervention method of Collaborative Story Craft (CSC). As the word "mediation" implies, the process involves an external actor who facilitates an exploration of stories (Fonseca Silva 2020). This requires bearing witness and validating individual narratives in relation to the object of work within the social and cultural scripts of a community of practice.

Story Mediation, as we know, requires familiarity with our concepts (CSA and CSC) and it is conducted by qualified Story Mediators who are trained to assist us in our practice. Alternatively, professionals and researchers who acquire the qualifications to appropriate our tools, can practice Story Meditation in the organisation that they belong to.

Through Collaborative Storytelling Activity (CSA), Story Mediators serve to actively listen to the storyteller by documenting, analysing, validating, and identifying the themes, patterns, and metaphors within the narratives and scripts of the workplace.

Both dialogue and documentation are important to Story Mediators and storytellers to keep standards and fulfil obligations of the work activities within "reasonable expectation" of the members (see accountability as documented storytelling by Boven et al. 2014, p. 3). In his book *Together: the rituals, pleasures and politics of cooperation*, Richard Sennet calls these activities "dialogic skills" (2013, p. 6).

The Story Mediator's main responsibility is not to tell the story, but rather help explore patterns of existing knowledge, opportunities, and challenges within individual lived experiences of roles, motivation, and purpose at work.

Story Mediation relies on sensemaking through the interplay among theory, practice, external narratives, and one's own story. In this fusion of "social worlds," the learning opportunities are extended beyond those being "served" as the Story Mediator is also affected by (and contributor to) the collective sensemaking process.

Story Mediation in Collaborative Storytelling uses the intervention tool Collaborative Story Craft to acknowledge an undertaking process of sensemaking through exchange, story creation (crafting), and story signification.

Collaborative Story Craft, as a pragmatic tool, helps map the "inventories" of stories and narratives in social worlds to facilitate dialogue amongst the actors to make sense and build collective stories together.

In the next chapter, the **work as craft mindset** is described as the foundation to Collaborative Storytelling to build narratives in organisational change. The work as craft mindset invites the reimagining of the past and a possible future through individual and collaborative stories.

Conclusions

Collaborative Storytelling Activity (CSA) aims to make sense of the nuances of multiple embodied and lived stories in relation to an activity with members of a community of practice as the storytellers. As a tool for Collaborative Storytelling, Story Mediators use the method of Collaborative Story Craft (CSC), which requires the engagement of those who influence and are being impacted by dominant narratives or hidden scripts at the workplace.

Story Mediators applying CSC within an organisational story support validating and developing the messages that resonate with the collective. Rather than telling the stories for those experiencing the story (the storytellers), Story Mediators' main intention is to facilitate an exchange of stories through dialogue and documentation to reveal the commonalities that align with a united purpose.

Notes

1. Similarly, Clifford Geertz (1973) calls this "thick description," which gives detailed descriptions and interpretations of situations observed by a researcher. Thick description involves writing detailed narratives or 'vignettes' explaining situations and their background 'context'.
2. "Thick description refers to the researcher's task of both describing and interpreting observed social action (or behavior) within its particular context" (Ponterotto 2006, p. 543).
3. In 2000, Alvesson and Kärreman argued that discourse analysis of empirical data could be recognised through two key dimensions: the relationship between discourse and meaning and (2) the attentiveness to detail of a specific context versus a more standardised form of language use. To explain this, the authors describe "climbing the ladder of discourse" between big "D" discourse and little "d" discourse (Cleland Silva 2019, p. 87).

References

Acker, Joan. 1990. Hierarchies, jobs, bodies: A theory of gendered organizations. *Gender and Society* 4 (2): 139–158.

———. 2006. Inequality regimes: Gender, class, and race in organizations. *Gender and Society* 20 (4): 441–464.

Alvesson, Mats, and Dan Karremän. 2000. Varieties of discourse: On the study of organizations through discourse analysis. *Human Relations* 53 (9): 1125–1149.

Aromaa, Eeva, Päivi Eriksson, Jean Helms Mills, Esa Hiltunen, Maarit Lammassaari, and Albert J. Mills. 2019. Critical sensemaking: Challenges and promises. *Qualitative Research in Organizations and Management: An International Journal* 14 (3): 356–376.

Bateson, Gregory. 1972. *Steps in an ecology of mind.* New York: Ballantine Books.

Boven, Mark, Robert E. Goodin, and Thomas Schillemans, eds. 2014. *The Oxford handbook of public accountability.* Oxford: Oxford University Press.

Cameron, Lynne, Graham David Low, and Robert Maslen. 2010. Finding systematically in metaphor use. In *Metaphor analysis: Research practice in applied linguistics, social sciences, and the humanities*, ed. Lynne Cameron and Robert Maslen, 116–146. London: Equinox.

Choudhury, Shakil. 2015. *Deep diversity: Overcoming Us vs. Them.* Toronto: Between the lines.

Cleland Silva, Tricia, and Paulo de Tarso Fonseca Silva. 2019. Validating change through collaborative story craft. In *Sage research methods cases part 2.* Thousand Oaks: Sage. https://doi.org/10.4135/9781526478245.

———. 2021. Collaborative story craft as a tool for inclusive workplace practices. In *History and storytelling in business*, ed. Albert Mills, Nick Deal, and David Boje. Singapore: World Scientific.

Cleland Silva, Tricia. 2019. Transnational management and globalised workers an: nurses beyond human resources. New York: Routledge.

Cortazzi, Martin. 2001. Narrative analysis in ethnography. In *Handbook of ethnography*, ed. Paul Atkinson, Amanda Coffey, Sara Delamont, John Lofland, and Lyn Lofland. London: Sage.

Diamond, Julie. 2016. *Power: A user's guide.* New Mexico: Belly Song Press.

Dnika, Travis J., and Jennifer Thorpe-Moscon. 2018. *Day-to-day experiences of emotional tax among women and men of color in the workplace.* Toronto: Catalyst. https://www.catalyst.org/wp-content/uploads/2019/02/emotionaltax.pdf.

Dnika, Travis J., Julie S. Nugent, and Courtney McCluney. 2016. *Engaging in conversations about gender, race, and ethnicity in the workplace.* Toronto: Catalyst. https://www.catalyst.org/research/emotional-tax-how-black-women-and-men-pay-more-at-work-and-how-leaders-can-take-action/.

Eshraghi, Arman, and Richard Taffler. 2015. Heroes and victims: Fund manager sensemaking, self-legitimation and storytelling. *Accounting and Business Research* 45 (6–7): 691–714.

Fachin, Fernando, and Ann Langley. 2017. Researching organizational concepts processually: The case of identity. In *The SAGE handbook of qualitative business and management research methods: History and traditions*, ed. Catherine Cassell, Ann L. Cunliffe, and Gina Grandy, 308–327. London: Sage Publications.

Fainsilber, Lynn, and Andrew Ortony. 1987. Metaphorical Uses of language in the expression of emotions. *Metaphor and Symbolic Activity* 2 (4): 239–250.

Fonseca Silva, Paulo de Tarso. 2020. The work of a story mediator: Writing the backstory of a profession. In *Power of story of power*. Austria: Beyond Storytelling.

Gabriel, Yannis. 2004. The narrative veil: Truth and untruths in storytelling. In *Myths, stories, and organizations: Premodern narratives for our times*, 17–31. Oxford: Oxford University Press.

Geertz, Clifford. 1972. Deep play: Notes on the Balinese cockfight. *Daedalus* 134 (4): 56–86.

———. 1973. *The interpretation of cultures*. New York: Basic Books.

Gibbs, Raymond W., Jr. 2013. Walking the walk while thinking about the talk: Embodied interpretation of metaphorical narratives. *Journal of Psycholinguistic Research* 42 (4): 363–378.

Goffman, Erving. 1959. The moral career of the mental patient. *Psychiatry* 22 (2): 123–142.

Greenhalgh, Trisha. 1999. Narrative based medicine in an evidence based world. *British Medical Journal* 318 (7179): 323–325.

Halverson, Jeffry, Steven Corman, and H. Lloyd Goodall. 2011. *Master narratives of Islamist extremism*. Switzerland: Springer.

Labov, William. 2013. *The language of life and death: The transformation of experience in oral narrative*. Cambridge: Cambridge University Press.

Lorino, Philippe, Benoît Tricard, and Yves Clot. 2011. Research methods for non-representational approaches to organizational complexity: The dialogical mediated inquiry. *Organization Studies* 32 (6): 769–801.

Madigan, Stephen. 2011. *Narrative therapy*. Washington: American Psychological Association.

Marshak, Robert J. 1993. Managing the metaphor of change. *Organizational Dynamics* 22 (1): 44–56.

———. 1996. Metaphors, metaphoric fields and organizational change. In *Metaphor and organizations*, ed. David Grant and Cliff Oswick, 147–165. London: Sage Publications.

Mindell, Arnold. 1995. *Sitting in the fire: Large group transformation using conflict and diversity*. Portland: Lao Tse Press.

———. 2002. *The deep democracy of open forums: Practical steps to conflict prevention and resolution for the family, workplace and world*. Charlottesville: Hampton Books.

Ng, Eddy S., and Greg J. Sears. 2020. Walking the talk on diversity: CEO beliefs, moral values, and the implementation of workplace diversity practices. *Journal of Business Ethics* 164 (3): 437–450.

Nin, Anaïs. 1961. *Seduction of the minotaur*. Chicago: The Swallow Press.

Ponterotto, Joseph G. 2006. Brief note on the origins, evolution, and meaning of the qualitative research concept thick description. *The Qualitative Report* 11 (3): 538–549.

Pritchard, David Brine. 1994. *The encyclopedia of chess variants.* UK: Games and Puzzles Publications.

Semino, Elena. 2008. *Metaphor in discourse.* Cambridge: Cambridge University Press.

Sennett, Richard. 2013. *Together: The rituals, pleasures, and politics of cooperation.* London: Penguin.

Shotter, John. 2006. Understanding process from within: An argument for 'withness'-thinking. *Organization Studies* 27 (4): 585–604.

———. 2010. Situated dialogic action research: Disclosing "beginnings" for innovative change in organizations. *Organizational Research Methods* 13 (2): 268–285.

Shukla, Nikesh (ed.) 2016. *The good immigrant.* UK: Unbound.

Smollan, Roy K. 2014. The emotional dimensions of metaphors of change. *Journal of Managerial Psychology* 29 (7): 794–807.

Snævarr, Stefán. 2010. *Metaphors, narratives, emotions: Their interplay and impact.* Amsterdam: Rodopi.

Strauss, Anselm. 1978. A social world perspective. *Studies in Symbolic Interaction* 1: 119–128.

Van de Ven, Andrew H. 2007. *Engaged scholarship: A guide for organizational and social research.* Oxford: Oxford University Press.

Weick, Karl E. 1995. *Sensemaking in organizations.* Thousand Oaks: SAGE.

Weick, Karl E., Kathleen M. Sutcliffe, and David Obstfeld. 2005. Organizing and the process of sensemaking. *Organization Science* 16 (4): 409–421.

White, Michael K. 1995. *Re-Authoring lives: Interviews and essays.* Adelaide: Dulwich Centre Publications.

———. 2007. *Maps of narrative practice.* New York: W.W. Norton & Company.

Yang, Jerry Austin, Audrey Boklage, Maximilan Kolbe Sherard, Christine Julien, and Maura J. Borrego. 2021. Cultural scripts, space, and identity: Perspectives of two LGBTQ+ engineering students on inclusive spaces. In *Collaborative network for engineering and computing diversity.* Washington: American Society for Engineering.

CHAPTER 3

Work as Craft Mindset: Building Narratives in Organisational Change

Abstract Storytelling is a craft. In this chapter, we explain why a *work as craft* mindset is essential to *Collaborative Storytelling* to make sense of work and to build narratives in organisational change. In particular, we discuss how storytelling is not only for an external audience but also a representation of who we are, what we do, and how we make sense of our relationships and environments. At the end of the chapter, we suggest *Collaborative Storytelling Activity System* as a way to approach work activity systems in a cultural historical context.

Keywords Activity systems • Cultural historical activity theory • Collaboration • Craft • Materiality • Organisational change • Storytelling • Sustainability • Tacit knowledge

> *...the strength of craft is in its essential humanity with all its delicious flaws and quirks.*
> —Sally Coulthard

Collaborative Storytelling is a multi-purpose activity that promotes the notion of work as craft mindset. This mindset proposes an alternative way of communicating and perceiving work during times of change. Having a

T. Cleland Silva, P. de Tarso Fonseca Silva, *Making Sense of Work Through Collaborative Storytelling*,
https://doi.org/10.1007/978-3-030-89446-7_3

craft mindset allows co-workers to make sense, "tinker with," and respond to different elements of the social worlds in which they belong and act in.

Craft is commonly understood as an activity that produces a unique handmade product which is based on the tacit knowledge of the craftsperson. Tacit knowledge of a craftsperson is learned in a community of practice and, through social interaction and lived experiences of the craft, the craft therefore is sensed by the body (Korn 2013; Victor and Boynton 1998).

The work as craft mindset is foundational to Collaborative Storytelling Activity which is an exchange of stories among co-workers, in relation to the work environment and its materiality. Story exchange in a cultural-historical context gives meaning to interpreting the past, present, and potential future, which German Philosopher Martin Heidegger describes as "being-in-the-world" as "absorbed, nondeliberative...practiced mastery [which relies on] skilled interaction with things and people" (Reimer and Johnson 2017, p. 1063).

Making Sense of Stories as a Craftsperson

The work as craft mindset is a way to reconnect with an authentic sense of purpose at the workplace as a starting point for collaboration. Collaboration is a "continued attempt to construct and maintain a shared conception of a problem" (Roschelle and Teasley 1995, p. 70) and a shared purpose of an activity. Work as craft mindset for collaboration is thus both an embodied individual experience and a moral stance about the stories and narrations embedded in the work system.

Craft itself is the basis from which all organisational knowledge is created (Victor and Boynton 1998, p. 24). The materiality of craft work provides clear goals and instant feedback. This sense of purpose (or fulfilment) anchors the craftsperson's understanding of reality and shapes their stories, ideas, beliefs, and identity, which organise their experience and influence their decisions (Korn 2013, p. 55).

Craftspeople rely on their tacit knowledge to materialise their visions, trusting that their body will respond to what needs to be done with their work. This ability to "trust" the holistic effort of mind and body in relation to the material environment activates not only the craftsperson's senses in a particular way but it also speaks to their sense of purpose at work.

Through cumulative tacit knowledge (Victor and Boynton 1998), each individual has a way to make sense, respond, and narrate their own experiences. Recounting these experiences does not necessarily prioritise or comply with "common sense," and they are often expressed through metaphors and stories. Even though it is difficult to explain, craftspeople know what to do at work. This "knowing" is more a reflection of their tacit knowledge than their ability to reason why they know.

Tacit knowledge is stored in the individual's mind and is a combination of experience, judgement, and intuition. Tacit knowledge is a powerful resource but difficult to share with others as it is gained and learned through "doing". Like riding a bicycle, tacit knowledge is easier to show rather than explain (Victor and Boynton 1998, p. 22).

The work as craft mindset extends beyond the traditional understanding of craft activities. The metaphor of work as craft (as opposed to craftwork) considers the process of making sense of work as an embodied experience in relation to tools and the material and social environment. This mindset harnesses judgment and problem-solving skills of the individual as part of a process of collective learning in a community of practice.

There is on-going feedback mediated by the tools and materials used by a craftsperson, which are channelled through senses. This real time response is dependent on the individual's own awareness as a unique embodied being. The close connection between body, tools, and environment also intensifies the craftsperson's sense of meaning and satisfaction, commonly understood as "being in the zone."

By proposing the metaphor of work as craft mindset, we hope to frame the perspective of collaborative work in organisations as a joint effort of individuality and craftsmanship. When a craft mindset is embodied, individuals can experience the materiality of their work in a particular way but also make sense and craft stories creatively and authentically. Therefore, work as craft mindset connects with the notion of what is being experienced at work through collaboratively telling and crafting stories during organisational change.

Craftsmanship and Metaphor: Expanding the Meaning of Organisational Stories

Collaborative Storytelling is a process and a joint effort that creates stories or builds on existing narratives within a group of individuals. Compared to other activities, mainly those activities that are centred on craftwork, storytelling "offers" stories as an "outcome" of the activity. In other words, engaging in storytelling implies that stories do not "materialise" out of nothing, as they embody a creative process in order to "become." We argue that anybody can tell stories, and they do, even without realising. When storytelling is a conscious process, it includes a creative effort and crafting through sensemaking, which is made by some "body."

The process of sensemaking and creation through collaboration embodied in Collaborative Storytelling Activity (CSA) was inspired by the second author's previous research on craftwork, which was framed through the study of "wooden boatbuilding activity."

The master thesis entitled "*Body, tools and the environment in craftwork: The study of wooden boatbuilding*" (Fonseca Silva 2017) explored craftsmanship from an embodied cognitive perspective. The objective of the research was to seek further understanding on the position of the body and its role in a craft activity by considering the use of tools and the material environment. The research considered the characteristics of the work environment that enabled the body of craftspeople to work more efficiently.
By having an embodied cognitive perspective (Lawrence 2012; Streeck et al. 2011), the research looked at the types of materials

(*Continued*)

(continued)
from the work environment that were selected and used for craft-work, and how material artefacts (tools) have contributed to the body's performance.
The research was associated with the Center for Research on Activity, Development and Learning (CRADLE) from the University of Helsinki and was initiated in 2013.
In the research, the craft work activity (wooden boatbuilding) was directed at building a replica of a gunboat—a big war vessel originally built in the eighteenth century in Finland as a Swedish territory. The first models of the vessel were designed for the Swedish–Russian War (1788–1790). The aim of the public funded project was to honour the history between Finland and Sweden by reconnecting with and promoting the craft of wooden boatbuilding (Fonseca Silva 2017, pp. 21–22).

It is fair to say that the outcome of the research mentioned above did not encapsulate the significance of that community of practice (wooden boatbuilding). Post reflections on the research redirected our interests to craftwork, eventually leading to what Collaborative Storytelling Activity (CSA) would become. The examples of craftsmanship portrayed in the research through wooden boatbuilding activity expanded the significance given to craftwork, literally and metaphorically.

By interviewing wooden boatbuilders and witnessing their work, it was possible to capture the essence of craft in practice. Each craftsperson had a particular way of preparing their work environment and organising their tools. Most importantly, each individual had a unique way to sense the materiality of their work, as the manifestation of their vision and their

Project manager: So, you have named your hammers [mallets]?
Wooden boatbuilder: *Yes. It's better because they have a bit… [They are] quite different…*
Researcher 2: What is its name?
Wooden boatbuilder (points): *"Petit" … [It is] the biggest one.*

(continued)

(continued)
Project manager: The biggest one?
Wooden boatbuilder: *Yes. Yes.*
Project manager: That is very... illogical.
Wooden boatbuilder (points): *Yes. And that is the smallest one.*
Researcher 1 (reading on the tool): Lazy...
Researcher 2 (reading on the tool): "Lazy hand."
Wooden boatbuilder: *But... It makes a lot of difference to have your own... sets [of tools]. Because... every set is a different set... The [caulking irons] (used with the mallets) ... they come from [a] black smith, so... Like, a black smith [makes them] so... they have a bit different angle and... (gestures with his hand to show the movement he does using the tool) ...you start to do like... all the time. You start to know how it works out* (Video interview, March 8th, 2013, in Fonseca Silva 2017, pp. 63–64).

(mental and physical) efforts. Above is an example of how wooden boatbuilders related to their tools.

The way that wooden boatbuilders cared for their tools was not only a reflection of how important the tools were for the work at hand. It also represented how important the established "relationship" was between the craftsperson's bodily senses and the materiality of the work environment. The established relationship was moved by a sense of purpose.

Based on this research, it was understood that when craftspeople do what they do best, their body, their tools, and the material environment become "one." This notion can be better described with the metaphor of "being in the zone." When that happens, the craftsperson's sense of self is extended to his or her tools, the material environment, and the object of work.

Although the materiality of the work can bring instant gratification to the craftsperson (feedback through the bodily senses and the material outcome of work), the value of craft, as we see, is not limited to the accomplishment of the object of the work or the financial rewards. Instead, the value of craft also resides in craftsmanship traditions, the lifestyle of the community of practice, and the embodied experiences that are validated through apprenticeship, the unique experiences of the craftsperson, and a sense of belonging to an activity system and a wider story.

While observing wooden boatbuilders at work was important for contextualising craft, listening to how they made sense of their work was even more revealing.

A lead craftsman narrated how being a craftsperson is like being an artist. He shared that, as soon as he arrived at the place where the gunboat would be built, he could "see" it ready, right in front of him. As a master in his craft, he mentioned that being a boatbuilder does not necessarily mean that one has to be equally good at sailing. Being a craftsperson means to "just know." He also used an example of a friend who makes musical instruments, but just recently had started learning how to play the guitar.
As a researcher, it was possible to witness a common concern among the craftspeople regarding their trade (wooden boatbuilding) losing its value or significance. Their narratives contributed to a story of conflict, where individuals, who loved their craft, struggled to justify why they remained in that profession, since other jobs could provide better financial stability to support their future and their families.
Another craftsperson revealed that although he had experienced other types of boatbuilding (with other materials than wood), no other work compared with wooden boatbuilding to him. He liked working with his hands, but he particularly liked how wood felt when he touched it with his hands and even how it smelled. Having a young family himself, he shared that his craft as a profession did not ensure the predictability he would like to have; however, he knew that he would not hesitate to favour wooden boatbuilding projects over another line of work, whenever the opportunities appeared (Field notes, Fonseca Silva, March 2013).

The craft work of wooden boatbuilders stood out for reasons that expanded from the work itself. That community of practice opened a pathway to the idea that craftsmanship is a lifestyle and a way of thinking. Having a work as craft mindset supports one's ability to respond to the environment, to solve problems, and to be present with what needs to be done at a certain time and place.

Having a strong sense of purpose towards an activity, belonging to a community of practice, and developing (and maintaining) a craft was clearly something that mattered to those craftspeople. Not only their narrative contributed to a bigger story but also their work could tell metaphorical stories. Their tools were given will, and their boats, each with a woman's name, carry many stories of apprenticeship and collaboration.

In a community of practice, material and narrated stories represent and propagate the work that should be agreed upon to become "storytelling material." In other words, in CoPs, stories should be crafted in collaboration to ensure that consent is part of the process.

Embodiment, action, and positioning in a material reality for a purpose or story is for us the context of *crafting* represented in Collaborative Storytelling Activity (CSA). Being exposed to stories in an environment of craft influenced our approach to what Collaborative Storytelling is today. It made us adopt a work as craft mindset in our story mediation practice. Most importantly, it initiated Collaborative Story Craft (CSC) as an intervention method to respond to the needs of people who are open to collaboration and willing to engage with their own stories for a meaningful connection with their work's purpose.

Story Crafting for Sustainable Change

The motivation of a craftsperson is intrinsic and extrinsic as the rewards are both material and emotional in nature (Coulthard 2019). With a work as craft mindset, the individual's contribution in the community of practice becomes anchored in the material and social reality of the work. This anchoring gives the opportunity for the organisational members to take pride and ownership in their role within that community.

Organisational change is an emotional and social process which involves conflicts and potential resolutions through consent and motivation of those involved (Bryant and Cox 2006). Exploring and discovering solutions to conflict can be socially, physically, and emotionally painful (like the concept of "emotional tax" introduced in Chap. 2). Ignoring the discomfort associated with change may prevent authentic commitment to a "new story" at work. Acknowledging the discomfort that comes with change will also include and speak to those being affected by the change. Without learning how organisational members relate to one another and to the on-going issues, the change will be reactive rather than sustainable (Mindell 1995).

Relating and connecting to each other is a craft. It involves a process of sensemaking of change as an embodied and individualised experience, influenced by the past, present, and potential future of relationships and the organisation's history and culture. Framing change with a work as craft mindset encourages the discernment of past and present patterns of working together, the purpose behind the work, and the material and social realities of the workplace.

We consider the mindset of craftspeople as both **thinkers and tinkers**.[1] Embodying that mindset at work means to set a well-defined intention and/or to envision a material outcome.

In practice, it also means to ask questions such as:

- *What do we need to do?*
- *What are we doing?*
- *What do I know about it?*
- *What do you know about it?*
- *How do we do it?*
- *What do we have to work with?*
- *Which tools do we need?*
- *Has anybody done this before?*
- *How did they do it?*
- *How can we do it better?* And so on.

By acknowledging and consenting to the reality as it is, collectively, rather than assuming what it may be, is one of the pre-conditions for Collaborative Storytelling. In other words, for Collaborative Storytelling to be authentic and sustainable in organisations, Collaborative Story *crafting* provides the appropriate mindset to act in a joint effort.

Crafting a common story as a process of sensemaking requires a common ground to begin with. In our work, we have experienced the influence of the metaphoric fields in everyday practices and relationships at the workplace, whether people are conscious of them or not. For example, a leader of a small company assumed "everyone is in the same boat" when it came to the future vision of the company. And yet, in reality, there were tensions between the members as the leader wanted to expand the company globally, whereas the others wanted the work activities to remain local with its original work purpose. 'Unpacking' the boat metaphor together provided an opportunity for the members to describe their emotions and embodied experiences by positioning themselves in reference to the boat. One member said they did not leave the shore and another was alone in a boat among many boats. Another member talked about not having a map or a clear sense of where the boat was going. As the members unpacked the metaphoric field with the leader, a lively discussion of sensemaking happened about past events and the potential future without assuming or projecting a dominant understanding of the organisational story (Cleland Silva and Fonseca Silva 2019).

David Grove called the process of questioning and becoming aware of implicit and explicit metaphors that we use to describe our experiences as "clean language" (Sullivan and Rees 2008). We acknowledge metaphors as valuable components for story craft as the metaphoric fields we navigate impact our minds, bodies, and imaginations at the workplace. Having a work as craft mindset is challenging to explain, but stories and metaphors serve as bridges to transfer meaning and knowledge to others who are willing to learn from another perspective.

In the following metaphorical story (which we translated and interpreted from Elena Bernabé[2]), we would like to illustrate the work as craft mindset. Our intention in choosing this story is to put into perspective the sensemaking of past and present experiences through body, mind, emotions, relationships, and place, which, in this story, is communicated beyond the tasks associated with craftwork.

The Grandmother and the Pain (La Abuela y el Dolor)

"Grandma, how do you deal with the pain?"
"With the hands, dear. If you deal with your mind, instead of relieving the pain, it will harden it even more."
"With the hands, grandma?"
"Yes, our hands are the antennas of our soul. If you move them by sewing, cooking, painting, playing or sinking them into the ground, you send signals of care to the deepest part of your being. And your soul brightens because you are paying attention to it [the soul]. Then the signals of the pain are no longer necessary."
"Are the hands really that important?"
"Yes, my girl. Think about babies: they start to know the world thanks to the touch of their little hands. If you look at the hands of older people, they tell more about their lives than any other part of the body.

(*Continued*)

(continued)
Everything that is handmade, so it is said, is made with the heart because it really is: the hands and the heart are connected.
Masseuses know this very well: when they touch another person's body with their hands, they create a deep connection. It is precisely from this connection that we reach the heart. Think about lovers: when their hands touch, they make love in the most sublime way."
"My hands, grandma... how long have I not used them like this!"
"Move them, my love, start to create with them and everything inside you will change. The pain will not pass but will transform into the most beautiful masterpiece. And you'll no longer feel the pain. Because you will have been able to transform its essence."

Before reading our interpretation of this story (in relation to work as craft mindset), take a moment to engage with your own interpretation of the story from your context and story as a learner. Consider the significance of the elements mentioned in the story (e.g., pain, hands, transformation, heart, and soul) and the characters (grandmother and granddaughter). How does the story speak to you?

For us, this metaphorical story conveys the connection of doing things (represented by the use of hands) and the reason given to work as a part of a wider purpose (such as transforming pain and teaching a child about self-care). The story connects with the significance of metaphors: speaking of one thing (hand work) in terms of another (dealing with pain holistically). The message of this metaphorical story, to us, gives the idea that we live a holistic existence in which the purpose is not restrained to one type of experience or work. Rather, any type of work affords sensemaking that goes beyond the task at hand, reminding us about our lived experiences as embodied, social human beings.

While our embodied experiences are unique and non-transferable to another person's experience (like the babies exploring the world with their little hands), stories invite others to explore different metaphoric fields and establish a more intimate connection between people (such as the grandmother and granddaughter of the story). The Grandmother's interpretation of pain can be extended to change. When given a deeper authentic purpose, change can be transformed into a "valuable masterpiece" rather than a "hardened" discomfort.

We interpret the metaphor of dealing with pain through one's hands as a way to expand the meaning given to an activity to a deeper existential purpose: pain does not disappear, but instead it is transformed.

As we acknowledge how uncomfortable change is, our sensemaking process continues to evolve and can be channelled through our (material) work with authenticity and purpose. As the grandma says to her granddaughter, "*the pain will not pass but will transform into the most beautiful masterpiece.*" Having a work as craft mindset in the story suggests that the sense of purpose is part of a sensemaking process: in other words, the granddaughter should embrace her senses in a material environment through her embodied connections, physical movement, and relationships with others. This is represented in the story as our hands being "*the antennas of our soul.*"

Craft facilitates self-awareness of our social context and lived experiences in relation to others and gives possibility to change and develop ourselves as the process positions us to reflect on our knowledge, problem-solving skills, and state of readiness to change (Krugh 2014). Most importantly, self-awareness through the body and craft, gives the possibility for the collective to change together by considering the dynamics of power within a group. Paulo Freire calls this self-awareness process "conscientização" (conscious-raising or critical consciousness), which involves reflecting on existing deep collective and shared knowledge that has emotional and politically powerful potential (Freire 1970).

Consciously Moving through Conflict: Cultural Historical Activity Theory

As an interdisciplinary approach to human sciences, Activity Theory originated in cultural- historical psychology, which was initiated by Alexei Nikolaevich Leont'ev, Lev Semyonovich Vygotsky, and Alexander Romanovich Luria. These psychologists believed that learning takes place through social interaction, mediating tools that are represented in signs and symbols, and a cultural historical environment. The mediating tools shape the way humans interact with reality and reflect the experiences and development of an activity within a cultural and historical place. Over the last 30 years, Activity Theory has been reconceptualised as Cultural Historical Activity Theory (CHAT) (Sannino and Engeström 2018) to situate the activity in a particular time and place.

CHAT uses "an activity" as a way to understand and explore organised systems in context. An activity, for this theory, is what a group does and has done, which is linked by a shared purpose. When the understanding of a shared purpose is challenged or when the activity comes into conflict with another activity system, the potential of change and development comes about by identifying and addressing the conflict retrospectively and collectively (Worthen 2014, pp. 58–61).

Within societal structures, there are numerous activity systems at work, and these systems can co-exist in the same community of practice and cultural historical context. According to Roth (2014), "[T]he collective aspect of activity theory is concretely realized by an individual at a specific cultural–historical time and place. Activity theory perceives motive-oriented activities as concretely brought about by means of conscious, goal-directed actions" (p. 25). With Marxist roots, CHAT takes a political stance of the goal-directed actions of work (e.g., solely for profitable production) and their subsequent material consequences for the workers. Some goals, CHAT as a theory argues, may enforce contradictive and problematic ways of interpreting and doing the activity leading to dissatisfaction of the workers (Sannino and Engeström 2018). For example, in the 1980s, Finnish cleaners, who were trained and influenced by a historical model of craft-like home cleaning, had "bad conscience" when their everyday actions as cleaners was impacted by a dominant model of mass production. The workers lost meaning and pride in their work as they "repeatedly expressed their dissatisfaction with the kind of cleanliness they were able to achieve in their work" (Sannino and Engeström 2018, p. 47).

Another situation of applying CHAT could be elementary school teachers who have a shared purpose of providing an education to young children (the activity) in the school (cultural-historical context) in which they all teach. The teachers' activities are regulated by certain rules and norms; they have material tools to do their work (e.g., classrooms, grading systems) and they are regulated by larger societal structures of how education should be provided and with which resources. However, if the context changes or another activity system comes into conflict with the shared purpose, the teachers are challenged to change/develop their approach to continue engaging with the activity in a purposeful way.

A cultural-historical conflict (e.g., a global pandemic like COVID-19[3]) that challenges traditional ways of teaching illustrates the impact of context and other activity systems on the teachers' shared purpose. Not only does the pandemic conflict with how and where the teachers engage with their work activity but also the rules and expectations based on societal structures and other activity systems such as governing, parenting, and learning.

As activity systems are bounded by the activity's shared purpose, if something contributes to the shared purpose or object of the activity, then it is inside the activity system. If not, then it is outside the system, is part of another activity system, and/or comes into conflict with the system itself. When conflict occurs between activity systems that are driven by shared purposes, the conflict is political as the clash is defined by the motivation behind the purpose (Worthen 2014, p. 62). Broadly speaking, Cultural Historical Activity Theory "proposes that change and development (learning is change and development) takes place through workings-out of disagreements and conflicts" (Worthen 2014, p. 61). When the conflict is addressed and resolved, there are possibilities for a shift of power to occur or a stalemate, where the problem remains unresolved.

To understand the complexity of cultural historical activity systems and when conflict occurs through social interaction of multiple perspectives and networks of interacting activity systems (Engeström 2001, pp. 55–56), Engeström first mapped out a model structure in his 1987 dissertation *Expanding by Learning*. Below is our rendition of the model and a description of the various components: subjects, object & outcome, tools, rules, community, and division of labour (Fig. 3.1).

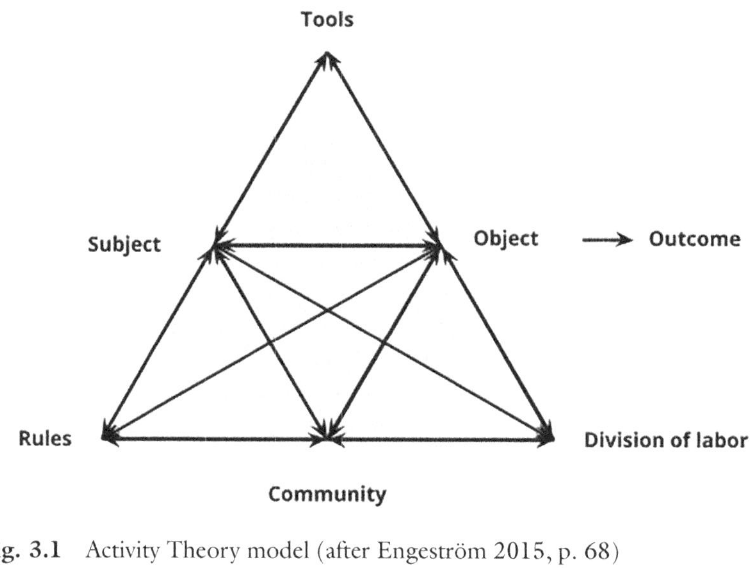

Fig. 3.1 Activity Theory model (after Engeström 2015, p. 68)

In CHAT, the *subjects* are those directly acting on the main objective of an activity. By acting on an *object*-oriented motivation, an *outcome* is expected.

Using teaching as an example of an activity, teachers are categorised as *subjects*, teaching a certain topic is the *object* and learning is the *outcome.*

Tools are social artefacts that "mediate" the activity in order to accomplish the common goal (object). As such, they not only mediate previous knowledge but also mediate the abilities of the subjects by either enabling or enhancing their performance in the activity. Whenever new tools are introduced in an activity, the activity transforms (Hasan 2002, pp. 135–136).

Depending on the context, the *subjects* are influenced by history, customs, laws, and regulations that surround the activity, which in the activity system model, is represented by *rules.*

The *community* is represented by all the actors directly or indirectly involved with the object of work within an activity.

The *division of labour* frames the responsibilities of various actors in relation to a common *object.*

As actors of an activity, the *subjects* and the *community* interact in a context (cultural and historical time and place). By analysing each of the elements (subjects, tools, object and outcome, rules, community, and division of labour) and their relationship as part of an activity system enables CHAT to be what it is.

The possibility to position the subjects as agents of change, having an overview of their reality also contextualises the emerging narratives of the activity that may contribute to or limit a particular organisation's story.

Collaborative Storytelling Activity System: Learning by Exchanging Stories

Collaborative Storytelling Activity System (CSAS) with a work as craft mindset, like Cultural Historical Activity Theory (CHAT), acknowledges power dynamics (culturally and socially embodied), and the responsibilities of each individual. CHAT helps to map an exchange of stories within a context and time frame, including making sense of an activity system for retrospective understanding and future possibilities of the collective activity. Reimagining the past through Collaborative Storytelling as craftspeople emboldens a disruption to established ways of organising (Suddaby et al. 2019) and puts into practice remembering a suitable past and constructing together a believable future for the community (Misztal 2003, p. 17).

Collaborative Storytelling Activity System builds on CHAT to explain how metaphoric fields and systems of narratives interweave with activity systems within a cultural and historical context of power. CHAT guides us to redirect "our gaze from what is going on inside the individual to what happens between human beings, their objects, and their instruments when they pursue and change their purposeful collective activities" (Sannino and Engerström 2018, p. 44). Collaborative Storytelling Activity System, on the other hand, is an invitation to reverse our gaze back to the individual as the starting point for expanding the understanding of the activity, and at the same time, not isolating the individual from being exposed to collective realities. Focusing on the commonalities among the interpretations of a shared activity speaks to an unconscious desire ignited in storytelling: to identify patterns and metaphors that relate to the stories within us.

CHAT has inspired research and practice resulting in the creation of intervention methods such as Change Laboratory (CL), which relies on the identification of tensions and contradictions within an activity system for analysing the conditions for developing the work (Sannino and Engerström 2017). We acknowledge CHAT as the basis of our work and Change Laboratory as a major influence in our intervention method: Collaborative Story Craft (CSC).

Change Laboratory (CL) is an activity theory-based methodology developed in 1996 (Engeström et al. 1996). CL is a process to implement the cycles of expansive learning defined by Yrjö Engeström in 1987 (Engerström 2001, 2015). CL, as an intervention, is used to study the conditions of change and to help those working in organisations to develop their work, drawing on the researcher's participant observation, interviews, and the recording and videotaping of meetings, and work practice (Engerström 2005).

Building on CHAT through the Collaborative Storytelling Activity System proposes that every activity system is also driven by stories (cultural, historical, and contextual to the activity). This framing also reminds us that storytelling as an activity is connected to an audience. We consider

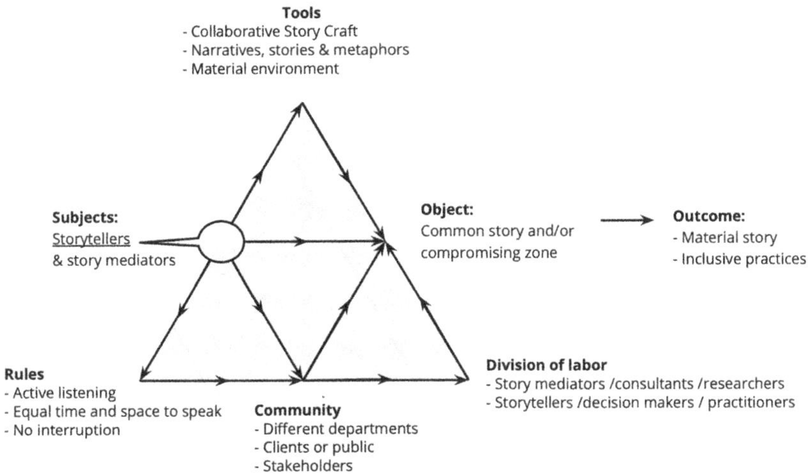

Fig. 3.2 Collaborative Storytelling Activity System Model

each member of an activity system as storytellers whose narrations are the starting point of analysis and give significance and meaning to how, by whom, and in what ways the work is done (Fig. 3.2).

When a Collaborative Storytelling Activity System is incorporated into another activity supported by Story Mediators, the Collaborative Storytelling Activity System is considered an intervention and it is then called Collaborative Story Craft (CSC) (Fig. 3.3).

Collaborative Storytelling Activity System, therefore, intersects with CHAT and reframes the elements of the activity within an on-going story of a larger system of narratives. This allows easier pathways to investigate the actors who (historically) have had the opportunity to contribute to the activity's script. By reframing the activity system to welcome stories, we aim to include more voices and redistribute the power to tell and craft a joint version of the organisational story.

Conclusions

Collaborative Storytelling Activity with a work as craft mindset gives storytellers an opportunity to consciously discuss and engage with their work in a way that is witnessed and validated by their peers. Incorporating Storytelling Activity in the organisation's main activity system through Collaborative

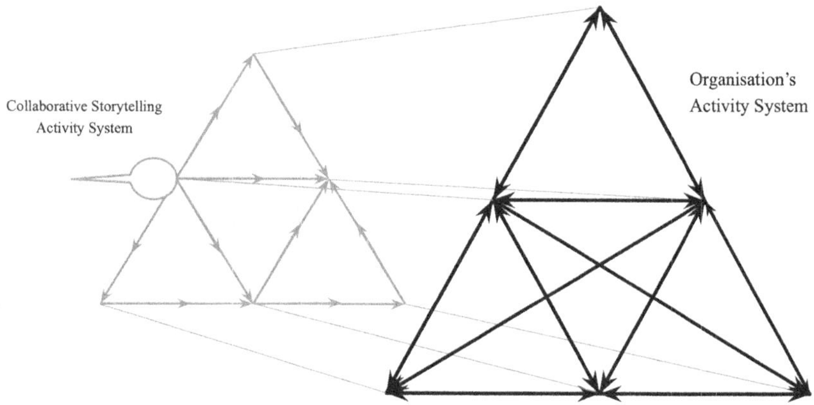

Fig. 3.3 Collaborative Storytelling Activity System incorporated into the activity system of an organisation

Story Craft enables a collective effort that includes the interpretations of members in a community of practice on their craft through Story Mediation. Opposed to focussing on tension and contradictions, Collaborative Storytelling highlights common themes that unite the actors for building an inclusive narrative. This approach acknowledges the cultural-historical context of the work activity through an intersection of narratives and several embodied identities. It also opens a channel of communication where multiple voices can contribute and consent to the development of a story, which will later be materialised in the rules and regulations for change.

Notes

1. We found allyship with other tinkers of organisational studies. Eva Boxenbaum and Linda Rouleau discuss new knowledge products as bricolage (tinkering) by exploring metaphors and scripts in organisational theory for *Academy of Management Review* 36, no. 2 (2011): 272–296.
2. Elena Bernabé (2020) "Abuela, ¿como se afronta el dolor?" *Crónicas de la Tierra sin Mal.* URL: https://cronicasinmal.blogspot.com/2020/08/el-dolor-como-afrontarlo.html?spref=fb&m=1
3. Ann Langley uses the case of COVID-19 to discuss process theory creation during disruptive times. She uses metaphors to frame process thinking in relation to COVID-19 as evolution, narrative, activity, and witness. Source: 2021. "What Is "This" a Case of? Generative Theorizing for Disruptive Times." *Journal of Management Inquiry* 30 (3): 251–258.

References

Bernabé, Elena. 2020. Abuela, ¿como se afronta el dolor? *Crónicas de la Tierra sin Mal.* https://cronicasinmal.blogspot.com/2020/08/el-dolor-como-afrontarlo.html?spref=fb&m=1.

Boxenbaum, Eva, and Linda Rouleau. 2011. New knowledge products as bricolage: Metaphors and scripts in organizational theory. *Academy of Management Review* 36 (2): 272–296.

Bryant, Melanie, and Julie Wolfram Cox. 2006. The expression of suppression: Loss and emotional labour in narratives of organisational change. *Journal of Management & Organization* 12 (2): 116–130.

Cleland Silva, Tricia, and Paulo de Tarso Fonseca Silva. 2019. *Validating change through collaborative story craft. SAGE Research Methods Cases Part 2.* Thousand Oaks: SAGE.

Coulthard, Sally. 2019. *Crafted: A compendium of crafts: New, old, and forgotten.* London: Hardie Grant Publishing.

Engeström, Yrjö. 2001. Expansive learning at work: Toward an activity theoretical reconceptualization. *Journal of Education and Work* 14 (1): 133–156.

———. 2005. *Developmental work research: Expanding activity theory in practice.* Berlin: Lehmanns.

———. 2015. *Learning by expanding.* Cambridge: Cambridge University Press.

Engeström, Yrjö, Jaakko Virkkunen, Merja Helle, Juha Pihlaja, and Ritva Poikela. 1996. The change laboratory as a tool for transforming work. *Lifelong Learning in Europe* 1 (2): 10–17.

Fonseca Silva, Paulo de Tarso. 2017. *Body, tools and the environment in craftwork: The study of wooden boatbuilding.* Helsinki: University of Helsinki.

Freire, Paulo. 1970. *Pedagogy of the oppressed.* New York: Continuum.

Hasan, Ruqaiya. 2002. Semiotic mediation, language and society. Three exotripic theories-Vygotsky, Halliday and Bernstein. In *Language, society and consciousness: The collected works of Ruqaya Hasan*, vol. 1. London: Equinox.

Korn, Peter. 2013. *Why we make things and why it matters: The education of a craftsman.* New Hampshire: David R. Godine.

Krugh, Michele. 2014. Joy in labour: The politicization of craft from the arts and crafts movement to Etsy. *Canadian Review of American Studies* 44 (2): 281–301.

Langley, Ann. 2021. What is "This" a case of? Generative theorizing for disruptive times. *Journal of Management Inquiry* 30 (3): 251–258.

Lawrence, Randee Lipson. 2012. Intuitive knowing and embodied consciousness. *New Directions for Adult and Continuing Education* 134: 5–13.

Mindell, Arnold. 1995. *Sitting in the fire: Large group transformation using conflict and diversity.* Portland: Lao Tse Press.

Misztal, Barbara. 2003. *Theories of social remembering.* UK: McGraw-Hill Education.

Reimer, Kai, and Robert B. Johnson. 2017. Clarifying ontological inseparability with Heidegger's analysis of equipment. *MIS Quarterly* 41: 1059–1081.
Roschelle, Jeremy, and Stephanie D. Teasley. 1995. The construction of shared knowledge in collaborative problem solving. In *Computer supported collaborative learning*, 69–97. Berlin: Springer.
Roth, Wolff-Michael. 2014. Reading activity, consciousness, personality dialectically: Cultural-historical activity theory and the centrality of society. *Mind, Culture, and Activity* 21 (1): 4–20.
Sannino, Annalisa, and Yrjö Engeström. 2017. Co-generation of societally impactful knowledge in change laboratories. *Management Learning* 48 (1): 80–96.
———. 2018. Cultural-historical activity theory: Founding insights and new challenges. *Cultural-Historical Psychology* 14: 43–56.
Streeck, Jürgen, Charles Goodwin, and Curtis LeBaron. 2011. *Embodied interaction: Language and body in the material world*. Cambridge: Cambridge University Press.
Suddaby, Roy, Diego Coraiola, Charles Harvey, and William Foster. 2019. History and the microfoundations of dynamic capabilities. *Strategic Management Journal* 41: 530–556.
Sullivan, Wendy, and Judy Rees. 2008. *Clean language*. New York: Crown House Publishing.
Victor, Bart, and Andrew C. Boynton. 1998. *Invented here: Maximizing your organization's internal growth and profitability: A practical guide to transforming work*. Boston: Harvard Business School Press.
Worthen, Helena. 2014. *What did you learn at work today? The forbidden lessons of labour education*. New York: Hardball Press.

CHAPTER 4

The Work of Story Mediators

Abstract In this chapter, we describe how we work as Story Mediators to facilitate authentic story exchange for making sense of social identities and embodied realities at work. Starting with our own personal and professional stories, we discuss how we enter the workplace with our own embodied lived experiences. In addition, we share how our defined values help us keep accountable to other storytellers and ourselves.

Keywords Accountability • Emotions • Personal stories • Sensegiving • Sensemaking • Workplace • Values

No dress rehearsal, this is our life
—Ahead by a Century, The Tragically Hip

Starting with Personal Stories

We are writing this book as academic practitioners and co-founders of a consulting business, but our partnership started as a married couple. With all our social identities as individuals, we also have embodied the identity of members of a multicultural family. While this identity did not seem to matter when we first met, as our relationship grew, we sensed a shift of the existing narratives regarding who we were. This realisation led us to the stories we wanted to claim, to nurture, and ultimately craft together. The

T. Cleland Silva, P. de Tarso Fonseca Silva, *Making Sense of Work Through Collaborative Storytelling*,
https://doi.org/10.1007/978-3-030-89446-7_4

freedom of choosing one's own story was a recurring theme that we did not want to take for granted.

In 2012, after the birth of our first child, Paulo started to wonder about his daughter's social identity. He asked himself, will she be Finnish, Brazilian, or Canadian? Out of this question, he started to wonder about his own story, which also included stories about his family and Brazilian culture. One particular story that he recalled from his childhood was about his grandmother's handmade doll. Solely by asking her the question, "When you were young, what did you play with?", a story was told with the movement of her hands about a doll made with fabric and straw.

The story had evoked a sense of pride in the grandmother, which was manifested when she explained how she had creatively sewed the hands of the doll to give an illusion of fingers. The story also had a nostalgic feeling to it, as the doll would later be given to a younger sister, soon after she got married, leaving her family home at the age of nineteen, and migrating to the south of the country. That was her only toy.

As a child, listening to the detailed story, Paulo could also see his grandmother as a child. The nostalgic feeling was contagious as he imagined her embodied lived experience of creating this doll in a time and place. It was a "place" that she would never relive, and he would never experience and yet both of them found themselves there, through story. The generation gap suddenly seemed to be shortened and other differences became irrelevant.

The story of the grandmother's doll was a reminder about Paulo's cultural "treasure." The story validated the importance of stories for one's identity and it could be passed on to his children. He knew that everyone had a mining field that could be explored. Being a treasure hunter in this field means to explore the hidden stories that could be valuable for answering a question, reconnecting with one's authentic identity, or building on a bigger purpose.

Motivated by our desire to make sense of our own stories, we started sharing our ideas with friends and others who were part of our social worlds at this time. What we discovered was that by holding space and actively listening to the storyteller, there was a physical and emotional response of pride, acceptance, and release of the teller for being witnessed and heard. By asking questions related to the story, rather than our own predefined questions, and then, on another occasion, validating the stories back to the teller, there was a shift which led to a new level of rapport. Many storytellers cried and/or listened with silent attention as they had their stories mirrored back to them, rediscovering multiple stories that make up their sense of identity. In this early stage of story mediation, we called ourselves "treasure hunters" as we explored and uncovered precious stories with the tellers.

Ever since we took the conscious path of working with stories, we have experienced the benefits of storytelling and story crafting in our professional life and as a multicultural family. Metaphora International, our company, is the result of the tools we have researched and developed over the years for enabling people to craft stories that speak to oneself and others. Our work as Story Mediators is an extension of our lifestyle, which values wellness, education, storytelling, and community.

While writing this book, the importance of sharing our own stories became clear because, as Story Mediators, we can only interpret the world from our own positioning and draw from our metaphorical stories to give meaning to what is going on (Cleland Silva 2021). This means that our research, writings, and storytelling are just mere reflections of our preexisting understandings, which are created and maintained through our senses (Geertz 1972, p. 86). It also reveals a profound sense of power and responsibility as to how stories are told, received, and spread to larger audiences.

Regardless of the size of the audience, storytelling evokes emotions, and those emotions affect people in unique ways—the storyteller and the story receiver. By acknowledging the power afforded to stories and the potential effects of storytelling, we have established in our practice that for Collaborative Storytelling to happen, a conscious exchange must take place. Exchanging stories does not mean any story. The stories must come from a place of authenticity. Only then, they will carry value that others will appreciate.

Although personal stories can make the storyteller feel exposed and vulnerable, they also make him or her more relatable to others as human beings—with limitations and challenges, aspirations and dreams. It takes courage to share anything personal and that in itself does not go unnoticed by the audience.

On the other hand, tapping into one's own vulnerability through personal stories does not mean to blindly trust the audience and hope for the best scenario. The storyteller must have clear intentions on what the story should communicate to a particular audience in a particular context, such as at work. Before sharing a personal story, the storyteller must also seek to empathise with the audience and take responsibility on how the story may land on others.[1]

As Story Mediators, we facilitate story sharing activities around themes within a context and related to an original intention (of the individual, organisation, or a common interest of a group). Mediating the stories, we discovered dominant themes related to purpose and belonging to a community of family, friends, and co-workers. Indeed, people wanted to know that their stories mattered, but most importantly, they wanted their stories to connect with others and contribute to a larger, collective purpose. One specific place that connects people socially, physically, and materially is the workplace.

Entering the Workplace as Story Mediators

Story mediation is an intervention method for collaborative sensemaking at work during times of strategic change. Most often, strategic change is not about sensemaking of individual members, but rather sensegiving by the leaders through narratives (Logemann et al. 2019). Sensegiving is a process attempting "to influence the sensemaking and meaning constructions of others towards a preferred redefinition of organizational reality" (Gioia and Chittipeddi 1991, p. 442). Indeed, sensegiving can facilitate the construction of shared accounts among members (Mantere et al. 2012), fostering positive attitude towards change (Stensaker et al. 2008). And yet, leaders may mistake their sense-giving influence on the members' sensemaking of the change (Kraft et al. 2018) as well as the emotional and material consequences when the sensegiving is contested (Maitlis 2005).

As Story Mediators, we begin the Collaborative Storytelling Activity with sensegiving actors to explore the present dominant narratives and metaphors at the workplace during the specific time of change. At this stage, from our social positions in the context, we are also sensegiving through our narratives as to who we are and what we are doing in the workplace. This sense-giving is an entry point for us to gain legitimacy, consent, and trust[2] to start the process of externalising individual members' stories but also familiarise ourselves with potential dominant narratives and sensegiving of the decision makers. In this respect, we are sensegiving to Collaborative Storytelling Activity to build narratives in organisational change by starting with the dominant group of actors. Once we receive consent by the dominant sensegiving actors and have a general view of the dominant narratives, we can start Collaborative Story Craft as an intervention.

Nonetheless, as external consultants, it is of vital importance that Story Mediators be aware of their position of power, especially regarding the perceptions of workplace actors. Story Mediators are in positions of perceived expertise, authority, and status which stem from how workplaces are approached and accessed by the external world. Through our consulting experiences, it is very easy to get passionate about the actors' stories or be charmed by a leader or a dominant actor in the group. We are not alone in this as power is fundamental to human existence and influences social interaction, interpretation, and behaviours, depending on the context (Diamond 2016, p.4; see Gherardi et al. 2007).

Self-awareness of power helps with understanding the force of narratives and metaphors in the workplace, but it also keeps us in check, so we do not misuse our authority and prevent marginalised or non-dominant stories from being included. There are two ways we strive to prevent the misuse of power when entering the workplace: (1) our mosaic of values called TILES, and (2) working with another Story Mediator who is outside the process of Collaborative Storytelling Activity with the organisation at that given time.

The mosaic of values (see at the end of book) is in Portuguese and English to reflect the co-founders' mother tongues and social identities. It also reflects where we practice Collaborative Storytelling Activity.

TILES: A Mosaic of Values

Our code of conduct is formed by a mosaic of values, referred to as **TILES**. Those values are connected with our story and how we expect to relate with our community of clients, collaborators, and partners in practice.

TRADE	INCLUSION	LIBERTY	EQUILIBRIUM	SUSTAINABILITY
TROCA	INCLUSÃO	LIBERDADE	EQUILÍBRIO	SUSTENTABILIDADE

While "trade, inclusion, liberty, equilibrium, and sustainability" are the values we promote externally (to potential clients), there are other values we incorporate into our collaborative practices.

T	*Trade, Time, Trust & Transparency*
I	*Inclusion, Intention & Information*
L	*Liberty and Leadership*
E	*Equilibrium (x 8 wellness dimensions)*
S	*Sustainable Stories*

It is important that every person or entity collaborating as qualified Story Mediators using Collaborative Story Craft (CSC) understands our mosaic of values (TILES) in its entirety.

Conclusions

When embracing the role of Story Mediator, practitioners should understand that stories, although resourceful information, should be respected as personal property.

Story Mediation validates (with the storytellers) that the stories captured by the Story Mediator are afforded the meaning that the storytellers intended. Most importantly, Story Mediators should get consent that the themes selected to be worked on as a group reflect the storytellers' contribution.

As receivers and witnesses of stories, Story Mediators are exposed to personal information and emotional manifestations of people's experiences. It is important to differentiate and guide the storytellers in their sensemaking process to consider the original intention of Collaborative Storytelling within a context (of an activity).

With work as craft mindset, Story Mediators rely on well-defined values that can address the impact that their role may cause in a community of practice. In our collaborative practices with other practitioners, our values also communicate our expectations when initiating a joint effort to mediate, research, or consult on Collaborative Storytelling Activities.

Notes

1. In regards to stories of individual trauma, unless the audience is composed of professional therapists who have consented to listen to "exploratory" personal stories, it is likely that both, the storyteller and the audience, will have an unpleasant experience—with no purpose or sense of direction. This is why it is important for the storytellers to reconnect the exchange with the original purpose and context of the activity while sharing stories.
2. Cornelissen and Werner (2014) discuss how framing of strategic change can invoke meaning in line with existing cultural understanding and to frame is to make things familiar to mobilise support and gain legitimacy for a change.

References

Cleland Silva, Tricia. 2021. "Big hat no cattle": Using multispecies metaphors to frame strategic HRM. In *Oxford handbook of animals in organisations*, ed. Lindsay Hamilton and Linda Tallberg. Oxford: Oxford University Press.

Cornelissen, Joep P., and Mirjam D. Werner. 2014. Putting framing in perspective: A review of framing and frame analysis across the management and organizational literature. *Academy of Management Annals* 8 (1): 181–235.

Diamond, Julie. 2016. *Power: A user's guide*. New Mexico: Belly Song Press.

Geertz, Clifford. 1972. Deep play: Notes on the Balinese cockfight. *Daedalus* 134 (4 Fall): 56–86.

Gherardi, Silvia, Davide Nicolini, and Antonio Strati. 2007. The passion for knowing. *Organization* 14 (3): 315–329.

Gioia, Dennis A., and Kumar Chittipeddi. 1991. Sensemaking and sensegiving in strategic change initiation. *Strategic Management Journal* 12 (6): 433–448.

Kraft, Anna, Jennifer L. Sparr, and Claudia Peus. 2018. Giving and making sense about change: The back and forth between leaders and employees. *Journal of Business and Psychology* 33 (1): 71–87.

Logemann, Minna, Rebecca Piekkari, and Joep Cornelissen. 2019. The sense of it all: Framing and narratives in sensegiving about a strategic change. *Long Range Planning* 52 (9): 101852.

Maitlis, Sally. 2005. The social processes of organizational sensemaking. *Academy of Management Journal* 48 (1): 21–49.

Mantere, Saku, Henri A. Schildt, and John A.A. Sillince. 2012. Reversal of strategic change. *Academy of Management journal* 55 (1): 172–196.

Stensaker, Inger, Joyce Falkenberg, and Kjell Grønhaug. 2008. Implementation activities and organizational sensemaking. *The Journal of Applied Behavioral Science* 44 (2): 162–185.

CHAPTER 5

Collaborative Story Craft: A Tool for Building Narratives in Organisational Change

Abstract In this chapter, we describe Collaborative Story Craft (CSC) as a tool for building narratives during organisational change. The chapter is divided into four parts: externalisation of stories, mirror materials, a workshop, and report. The workshop is structured around metaphoric fields to engage the practitioners. These fields are "Nurturing the Roots," "Occupational Well-being as a holistic story," and "Metaphorical Tourism." The metaphoric fields can be introduced on the same workshop day or spread over separate occasions, depending on the time and the size of the group.

Keywords Collaboration • Sensemaking • Craft • Intervention methodology • Occupational well-being • Organisational change

Collaborative Story Craft in Practice

A work as craft mindset through Collaborative Storytelling provides an opportunity to reflect and critically question current ways of working. Throughout history, craft has emerged as an alternative to mass industrial production and consumption based on profit (Luckman 2015). Craft comes from a desire for authenticity to give meaning to embodied, social experiences (Fine 2003) by drawing from past traditions and shared understanding of social and work life (Jasanoff 2015).

T. Cleland Silva, P. de Tarso Fonseca Silva, *Making Sense of Work Through Collaborative Storytelling*,
https://doi.org/10.1007/978-3-030-89446-7_5

When introducing Collaborative Story Craft (CSC) intervention to a workplace, Story Mediators simplify the description of the process by bringing the participants into a *craft mindset*, leading them into a metaphoric field with an invitation: "let's craft a story together." We also try to avoid the word "intervention" when conducting Collaborative Story Craft, in order to be in line with the choice of words from the "invitation" and to support the craft mindset.

The members of the organisation, taking part in the Collaborative Storytelling Activity through the Collaborative Story Craft intervention are primarily referred to as "storytellers."

As a supporting tool in processes of organisational change, CSC can lead to multiple parallel outcomes. It all depends on the intention established by the decision makers and how Collaborative Storytelling Activity relates to the main activity system of the organisation. For example, the object of work of the organisation's main activity may or may not be aligned with the object of work of different departments or even the object of work within a temporary project, such as a strategy for organisational change.

Although the object of an activity (or multiple intersecting activities) within an organisation can be complex, Collaborative Storytelling as its own activity has a clear object: to find a common story and/or to establish a compromising zone for collaboration towards a common purpose. In many ways, the process of finding a common story in a community of practice may reveal how individuals interpret what they do together and how they relate to one another (exchanging experiences, learning, and collaborating).

In its original form, CSC is conducted in four phases (Cleland Silva and Fonseca Silva 2019). With the first and second phases, each storyteller takes part in an individual session with a Story Mediator. The third phase consists of the workshop with one or more Story Mediators and members of the organisation as storytellers. The number of Story Mediators for a CSC intervention is a minimum of two throughout the process, while the number of storytellers may vary depending on the size and needs of the organisation. The recommended (maximum) number of storytellers in a workshop is 20.

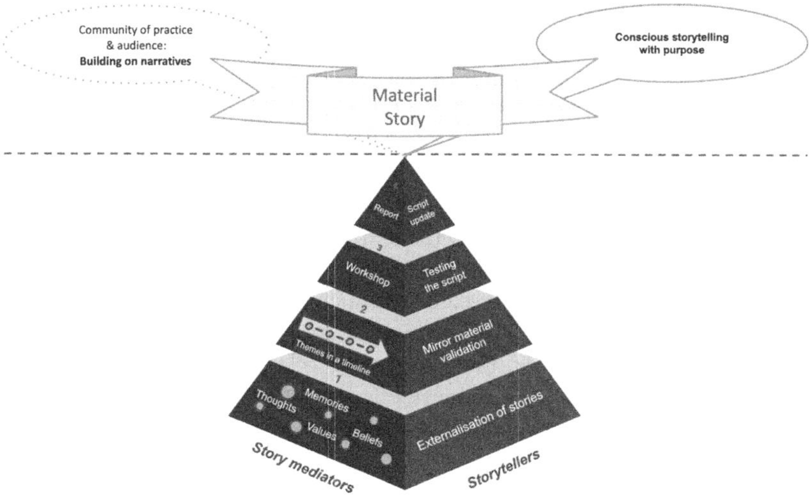

Fig. 5.1 Collaborative Storytelling Activity with the intervention tool Collaborative Story Craft

The sensemaking process of the CSC phases differs between Story Mediators and storytellers. The version of CSC in Fig. 5.1 represents what each role (Story Mediator or storyteller) should expect prior to the starting of the intervention.

This two-dimensional model aims to represent the storytellers' perspectives as well as the Story Mediators' perspective of the same Collaborative Storytelling process. This version was built on the original, (one dimensional) *Collaborative Story Craft* model (Cleland Silva and Fonseca Silva 2019, p. 10).

The horizontal line divides the phases of the process below as what we perceive as collaborative "story craft." It represents what needs to be explored, understood, selected, agreed upon, and officialised in order to represent the collective. Above the line is anything that is commonly perceived as "storytelling" or *material story*, such as what is intended to be publicly told, promoted, or sold.

After the CSC intervention, the *material story* is supported by the *updated script*, which, on an individual level, may lead to *conscious storytelling with purpose*. On an organisational level, the *updated script* builds on the community of practice's narrative and its audience.

Although intersecting, the focus of each individual during the process is influenced by the responsibilities of each role (not only during the development of CSC but also within the organisation). In addition, the various perspectives of the CSC method can range depending on whether or how the individual had been exposed to the method before. In summary, the two perspectives represented in this model focus on each role (storyteller and Story Mediator) associated with their responsibilities or commitments in the process of change through the activity of Collaborative Storytelling.

Story Mediators should guide the storytellers throughout the process, and this also makes Story Mediators familiar with the overall storyteller's perspective (not the specific individual experience but as it is presented in Fig. 5.1). In other words, the perspective of the Story Mediator starts from his/her sense of responsibility (also as a researcher, interventionist, facilitator, and consultant), and it requires focus on a particular dimension (or perspective) in the Collaborative Storytelling process. Story Mediators have to (1) understand how CSC can be used as an intervention tool, (2) lead the way for the storytellers, so that they can make sense and contribute to the process, and (3) consider the storytellers as their own audience[1] for the final report.

At the same time, the storyteller's perspective does not prevent him/her from being exposed to the Story Mediator's perspective. However, engaging in each phase of the CSC process

does not require that the storyteller follows how the Story Mediator conducts his/her responsibilities. This freedom enables the storyteller to prioritise his/her own story in order to relate it to the organisation and later make connections with the story of other organisational members.

Introducing Collaborative Story Craft to the Workplace

Once the Collaborative Storytelling Activity officially initiates, CSC intervention is introduced to the workplace through a circular model,[2] and it correlates with the undergoing organisational change. The circular model represents a cycle in the organisation's story as a whole. In order to make sense of the current cycle, everyone involved (Story Mediators and storytellers) will go through a four-step process that can lead to a fifth step (material story) or a brand new cycle of CSC with renewed ideas and an updated purpose (Fig. 5.2).

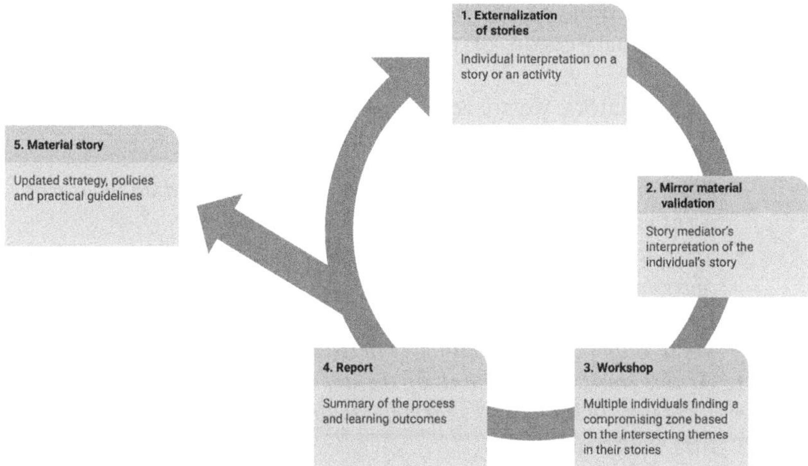

Fig. 5.2 Cyclical model of Collaborative Storytelling during organisational change with the intervention method of Collaborative Story Craft

Part One

Externalising Stories: Identifying Themes and Metaphors

Having a one-on-one session makes it easier to enable a safe environment to establish trust. It also initiates a story sharing mindset between the Story Mediator and the storyteller. For that reason, when externalising stories, there should be only one Story Mediator conducting the session, in order to diminish the amount of unnecessary stimulus or distractions.

For the storytellers, this phase means letting the ideas, memories, and opinions flow, orally. The elements of their narratives do not need to be structured in a certain way nor do they need to make complete sense. It is common that storytellers express their surprise regarding what they just told, not because it was anything new or too personal, but because it revealed something insightful that they did not anticipate before listening to themselves speaking aloud.

Each Story Mediator is the expert of his/her own craft, so he or she should select or prepare a set of lines to inform and reassure the storyteller about the process as a whole. The following lines came from our previous publication (Cleland Silva and Fonseca Silva 2019, p. 10) and they exemplify what we have used in our practice to explain and guide the storytellers at the first individual session of the CSC intervention (*externalisation of stories*).

As Story Mediators, we are responsible for taking notes, not to register

- *You will be able to craft a script for your story based on what you want others in the organisation to know about you.*
- *Your story is connected with the collective story and your ideas contribute to future strategies.*
- *I have no expectation on what you should tell.*
- *There is no right or wrong way to tell your story.*
- *At this point, it is normal for the story to be messy.*
- *I am here to listen and take notes so that we can help you to structure your story.*
- *Your story is yours to share and, as a storyteller, you can choose what you would like to share to others.*
- *We will not share your story without your consent.*
- *The workshop is the context in which you will be able to share your story.*
- *The themes in your story that connect with other participants' stories may influence the topics we address at the workshop. However, the identities of the storytellers whose themes were selected will not be revealed.*
- *In the next session, we can reinterpret the story together and select what is relevant to your story.*

everything that was shared (literally), but instead to capture moments in the narrative that, we felt, represented something important. In our practice, we identify recurring themes, metaphors, and the identification of a shift in the storyteller's emotions as important moments to take note.

In other words, Story Mediators hold space for the storytellers. They bear witness to the manifestation of the stories and the sensemaking process. It is a challenge to retain as much information as possible while showing genuine interest. However, this is also a sign that although Story Mediation can be taught, it does require a genuine interest in storytelling work through a craft mindset.

Considering that we all are storytellers (Cleland Silva and Fonseca Silva 2021), after the first session, Story Mediators also need to tell about the stories they have encountered as a way to make sense of their notes. This includes, especially, the interpretation they have afforded to the metaphors and the relations among the recurring themes. Therefore, after the individual session with the storyteller (of the organisation), the primary Story Mediator tells another Story Mediator about his/her impressions of the story that he/she received. In our practice, this storytelling activity, from one Story Mediator to another, is called "offloading."

Although the Cambridge dictionary's meaning of *offloading* refers to getting rid of something that you do not want by giving it to someone else, sharing the experience with another Story Mediator is not intended to get rid of the story or transfer the responsibility to another person. Instead, we aim to diminish our bias and the limits of our socially constructed lens. By having a second opinion and the opportunity to listen to our own thoughts aloud, both Story Mediators (primary and supporting Story Mediator) exchange ideas as to how the content for the potential "script" could be organised and structured. This potential "script" for the storyteller is also called *mirror material*, and it can be structured in a word document, PowerPoint slide, or any other way that can be later shared with the storyteller. The structure of the developing "script" takes into account the main themes or metaphors of the narrative as "chapters," which are placed in a chronological order.

Part Two

Structuring Themes and Validating Stories

This is the second (and last) individual session in a cycle of the CSC intervention. For the storytellers, this phase means that they get to listen to their own story in the Story Mediator's voice. The storytellers are usually very intrigued and curious about what the story has become from what they shared in the previous session. Without knowing, their emotions become more expressive, and it shows in the way they communicate while validating, correcting, or complementing the Story Mediator's interpretation of their story.

In this session, the Story Mediator also embodies a storyteller's role without losing sight of their own responsibilities with Story Mediation and the CSC method. Not only is the Story Mediator responsible for re-telling the story while seeking validation of the crafted mirror material but he or she also needs to be attuned to the storyteller's complementary information to the mirror material (soon to be script).

Following this session, the mirror material is updated by the primary Story Mediator and shared (only) with the storyteller. The storyteller will then have the freedom to continue building on the mirror material to fully appropriate its content to become a personal "script." The "script" then can evolve and the storyteller can work independently on his/her "script" for a particular context and audience. The first opportunity to try out the script with Collaborative Storytelling in organisational change is during a workshop alongside work colleagues (other storytellers) and the Story Mediators.

To prepare for the workshop, Story Mediators meet after the validation sessions are complete to compare how the content of different mirror materials intersect. Commonalities among stories, such as metaphors, will be given special attention, as they will help to structure the workshop: defining the major themes and tailoring the activities for that particular community of practice.

Part Three

Testing Scripts in a Workshop

Although there are endless possibilities for tailoring the workshop in relation to time and the themes of many stories collected and validated, there are "traditional" ways to structure the event(s). In ideal scenarios, the organisation would be prepared to participate in a six-hour workshop divided into three metaphorical fields that reflect the work in the past, present, and future. These fields are called (1) *Nurturing the Roots*, (2) *Occupational Well-being as part of a holistic story*, and (3) *Metaphorical Tourism.*

Nurturing the Roots

The "Nuturing the Roots" metaphor aims to signify origins such as how the stories at work have become what they are, starting from individual stories and how their paths have merged at the organisation. The metaphor also aims to reconnect to the stories of how work used to be before the change. The aim of this metaphor is to acknowledge different sources, inform how the organisation's story affects individuals, and validate that each story, as the representation of one's experience, is worth being listened to. Those stories, a lot of the time, are foundational to the feelings towards collaboration for the purpose of change.

The metaphor of "roots" reminds the group that although hidden, stories are important and even more present than they realise. Nurturing those stories does not mean to keep bringing the "roots" up, instead there should be an opportunity to learn the reasons why the root stories sustain the collective sense of identity in the organisational context. Nurturing the stories of before (in relation to now) links back to the origins of the organisation, its founders, and the work that was needed in order for the organisation to be what it is. Ultimately, the meaning proposed by Nurturing the Roots leads back to people and their stories as individuals.

Story Mediators are responsible for facilitating the discussion in a way that the exchange of stories is well-balanced with a fair amount of time to all participants. There are some guidelines that frame the type of stories that could be shared in that context and for that audience.

Reflect and take notes on the following topics:

1. **Your early story**: background, personality, and interests
2. **The path you have taken until now**: choices, studies, career
3. **Your connection**: what brought you here and how your story relates to this work

Story Mediators will give some time for the storytellers to think about the guidelines and craft a small script with the main topics that each individual would like to share.

Having gone through the two previous Story Mediation sessions (externalisation of stories and validation of stories), the storytellers can use the script that they had previously worked on to select the content that is appropriate for that workshop setting. There should be a time dedicated for each participant to be the storyteller and receive direct feedback from his or her peers.

While not telling a story, each participant should be an active listener [3] to provide resourceful but authentic feedback. To help with that, we ask the participants to follow some guidelines:

- How does your colleague's story relate to your story?
- What caught your attention in the story?
- Was there something significant that you didn't know about the person?

* *Take notes and consider some words of encouragement.*

With each storyteller's turn, there should be a round of feedback by the other storytellers. After the round of feedback, the storyteller can express his or her thoughts to the group regarding how his or her story had been received. In the meanwhile, Story Mediators can collect information that complements the overall themes, which later can be added to the final report.

Occupational Well-Being as Part of a Holistic Story

Our bodies and social identities experience work differently and uniquely. How we communicate and socially construct our physical and emotional needs as well as limitations are influenced by our social worlds and systems of narratives both inside and outside the workplace.

Describing physical and psychological needs at work can be difficult, especially as it can lead to vulnerable situations. To guide preparation for Collaborative Storytelling Activity, the Story Mediators introduce eight dimensions of experiencing wellness (e.g., Smith and Puczkó 2008 who describe six dimensions, p. 57) which are connected in a circle (see Fig. 5.3).

The storytellers are requested to rank these dimensions from top priority to least priority in relation to their lifestyle choices (Table 5.1). There are two ways that these dimensions can be ranked: (1) the current reality and (2) the ideal scenario. *The current reality* reveals which areas have been prioritised and which areas have been neglected. Whereas *the ideal scenario* informs what the preferences are in relation to a well-balanced and healthy lifestyle.

By ranking wellness dimensions, the storytellers get a chance to share their values and beliefs about their well-being, but also the stories that have influenced the choices in their lifestyle. For instance, in past workshops, storytellers passionately shared why one dimension means more

Fig. 5.3 The wellness dimensions: eight areas of physical and psychological wellness

than another, revealing a deeper understanding of how people socially and physically experience wellness in their lives. It also gives the storytellers an opportunity to explore their personal powers within their positions at work.

In May 2020, Tricia conducted a CSC workshop amongst multidisciplinary professional students of a master's in health business management. In relation to their work in the context of the global pandemic, COVID-19, the students ranked their wellness dimensions individually and then shared as a group.

The story exchange was lively to say the least. All 25 participants shared their rankings and described the reasons behind their list of wellness priorities. One conversation, in particular, revolved around

(*continued*)

(continued)
financial vs. spiritual dimensions, with one participant being unconvinced that finances should not be placed above all the other dimensions. He asked the group: "if one does not have material wealth, then how can the other dimensions be sustained?" Another participant replied that even when she did not have financial wealth, it was her sense of a bigger spiritual purpose that kept her feeling well and hopeful.

Table 5.1 General definitions of wellness dimensions in alphabetical order

Emotional Awareness of one's feelings, what those feelings are associated with and how they can be expressed.	**Occupational** A strong sense of working role and how this role is aligned with your calling, your values, your talents, and purpose.
Environmental Awareness of physical/natural surroundings and one's responsibility to care, maintain, or create an environment that enables a healthy/sustainable lifestyle.	**Physical** Recognising and proactively maintaining biological needs related with good nutrition, activity, and sleep for the body to function well.
Financial Feeling satisfied with the current and future financial situation and having a sense of control and ownership over resources.	**Social** Developing a sense of connection, belonging, and a well-established support system.
Intellectual Stimulated mind and the desire to learn new concepts, to improve one's skills, to be mentally challenged, and seek accomplishment.	**Spiritual** Being connected with a sense of meaning and expanding one's sense of purpose in life. Exercising wonderment and having a belief beyond one's own control.

Metaphorical Tourism

In this part of the workshop, the "tourism" metaphor taps into the meaning of "journey" but instead of giving a grand significance, such as "life's journey," it is used to signify the movement of ideas and stories about a reality that is not (currently) tangible. This Metaphor can be appropriated to different timelines.

What makes this a metaphorical *tourism* as opposed to a *journey* is that touristic trips are temporary. This reminds the "tourists" that they have a familiar place to come "home" to, meaning the current, non-imaginary reality, after exploring the new imaginary situation.

In the context of the workshop, it suggests a "visit" as to how the future could be. As mediators, we introduce Metaphorical Tourism as a follow up to build on the exchange that happened earlier in Nurturing the Roots. With that timing, Story Mediators propose an alternative meaning for the story exchanges. In addition to being *root* stories, we refer to previously "hidden" stories as stories that now have been "unpacked." In other words, *unpacked* stories suggest that the *storytellers* know more about one another because they shared some of the stories that they had been carrying in their personal *backpack*. Now, it comes the time to work together with a *shared luggage*, where the challenge is to choose where they want to go and what type of stories should be taken to the *destination* they will *visit*.

The destination represents the change, not as an unpleasant place to consider but just as a touristic destination (that one chooses willingly). Change, in this context, represents the ideal scenario. Perhaps, some of the *tourists* are more experienced than others, meaning that they know exactly how the ideal scenario should look like because they have visited the destination many times before, metaphorically. While other *tourists* have yet to conceptualise what the ideal scenario should look like.

In the "metaphorical trip," the Story Mediators serve as "tourist agents," and the storytellers prepare themselves for a collective trip towards an ideal future destination. To illustrate the activity, we suggest a single metaphorical luggage for group travel. The Story Mediators then facilitate the story exchange as to what stories could be brought along, and what should be left behind to avoid extra weight for the type of destination.

Packing the luggage together allows participants to express their interpretation of the future collective destination of the work activities, and what material objects (e.g., tools) and expectations (written or unwritten) should be brought along for the journey. With this process, new or reinvented tools and strategies of the work itself can emerge through interpretations of the metaphor (of the ideal destination) and the previous story exchanges.

Based on the model of Collaborative Storytelling Activity System (Fig. 3.2), the Story Mediator facilitates the discussion of packing the luggage by asking the storytellers to think about the following questions in relation to the work activities:

- What is your role at work and what do you need to fulfil that role?
- What is your destination/where do you want to get to?
- Who are you travelling with?
- How should the responsibilities be divided?
- The map: what type of rules and guidelines should be put into place?
- What type of tools or resources do you need?
- Who is part of your community? Think about the landscape that surrounds the journey.

Through packing the luggage, the Story Mediator helps the group identify commonalities, in the face of disagreements, towards a potential "compromising zone." This compromising zone is documented by the Story Mediators through the agreement of the group and the potential areas of development. This document is later presented to the group as a new material story based on the entirety of the CSC intervention.

An example of Metaphorical Tourism

In 2019, we conducted a one-day workshop with a gender equality consultancy who recently received external funding for a two-year project. The consultancy was credible with a strong reputation of past work on issues of gender equality at the workplace and within national policy-making. The external funding expanded the consultancy from the founder to a team of six individuals: three researchers, a project manager, and a social activist for LGBT+ rights. We were asked to facilitate the CSC workshop because the founder wanted to start the project as a team with clear expectations of the project purpose, objectives, and members' roles.

By exchanging stories in relation to the project, there were various commonalities in the stories that emerged such as higher education degrees in gender studies; searching for the "right path"; questioning the sense of purpose and financial stability through work; combining work with activism and equality values; and seeing their career paths as a "calling."

(*continued*)

(continued)

During the Metaphorical Tourism, with the support of the Story Meditators, the group identified that the consultancy is a platform for all of them and represents a larger community of activists that should be acknowledged and included. Within this "compromising zone" identified as the destination, rules were established on how to get there. Those rules included:

- *The consultancy should not be limited to the founder. Instead, the consultancy is a place where team members can work on common projects, but also exchange experiences and feel that they belong to a community.*
- *As a platform, the consultancy is a collection of combined skills that should be considered when designing new solutions or seeking out new projects. With that mindset, the work and the sense of purpose can be extended to a wider network/timeframe.*
- *As a community, the people working with the consultancy should consider promoting each other's work and career aspirations by valuing their areas of expertise as well as their interests and choices.*
- *As a community and a platform, the consultancy should be used as a reference point to connect people and generate new opportunities for the future.*

The guidelines of the journey became:

- *To be aware of what type of knowledge can be found within the consultancy's community, and how such knowledge contributes in practice to the work and benefits the community it serves. It should also consider different perspectives of gender research with a holistic view of what equality is.*
- *To clarify the methods: by knowing what the consultancy's community can offer regarding tools and skills. As a result, the team should craft a clear message and speak louder in all the "communities" or platforms that they also belong to.*
- *To consider the tone of communication and avoid criticism: how to tell the consultancy's story. The message should consider the audience that the consultancy is aiming at, who else they might be reaching, and the channels of distribution. Depending on those elements, the message must be crafted in a way that matches the audience's "language," allowing the story to be interpreted properly.*

Sensing the Change by Drawing the Destination

Within Metaphorical Tourism, storytellers craft the common metaphor of the destination through a drawing activity. With this activity, the storytellers are provided blank sheets of paper and coloured pencils. Once equipped, the Story Mediators instruct the storytellers to draw an image of the ideal destination and to position themselves with their community of practice as fellow travellers.

> This drawing exercise requires the participants to gather in a circle. Once the storytellers begin to interpret their understanding by drawing, we ask the storytellers to pass their unfinished drawing to their neighbour to continue the interpretation. Each storyteller is then instructed to continue someone else's creation by adding their interpretation to the drawing.
>
> This request of letting go of one's drawing not only surprises the storytellers but also puts into perspective that a craft mindset should also be prepared for unpredictability. Passing the drawing around gives others a chance to craft the same artefact collectively.
>
> Once each drawing is passed to all the storytellers, the original drawing is returned to the one who started it. The storytellers then have an opportunity to exchange stories as to what they intended to draw at first and how they interpreted the collaborative outcome of the drawing.
>
> The storytellers' interpretation considers their role in the community of practice and the significance of the change as a metaphorical destination.

Although talking is helpful in collective sensemaking, exploring alternative ways of expression (e.g., through art) can deepen imaginary possibilities leading to creative solutions. With a work as craft mindset, storytellers use their senses to communicate their interpretation of the future destination of the work based on their imagination and embodied lived experiences. The embodied lived experience is associated with a common metaphor (change as destination and/or any other metaphor that emerged in the previous CSC phases).

Like craftwork, testing out our individual scripts and applying a common metaphor to the work present opportunities to learn. Drawing the ideal destination fosters the imagination to better understand how the scripts and metaphors as new tools can help do the work better together. In other words, in times of change, using the crafted scripts and a metaphor serves as a catalyst to imagine what future work could be like as a community of practice.

With a work as craft mindset, testing out the new scripts and metaphors most often begins with frustration or "breaking the mold of fit-for-purpose" (Sennett 2008, p. 210). And yet, this frustration has rich potential of "telling yourself something you know can be other than you assumed" (Sennett 2008, p. 11), and the humility of "coming-to-grips" that unresolved issues of the tool and work may remain unresolved (Sennett 2008, p. 154).

In some workshops, because of time limitations, the drawings are completed solely by the storyteller, who later shares their interpretation with the group. Below are two pictures of a CSC workshop based on the interpretation of a digital platform called the Health Village (as the metaphorical destination).

The first drawing was created by a former patient who was asked to serve as an expert member in building the Health Village. He interpreted his experiences without the digital platform, and his subsequent work contribution to the Health Village.

The person with an arrow in the head represents himself when he had a stroke. The maze represents the physical pain of rehabilitation as well as the emotional pain of getting information on how to heal from the stroke. The bike on the other side of the maze represents a return to "normal" or gaining strength to do previous activities before the stroke. The former patient communicated that to get to the bike, there should be more teamwork within the group to acknowledge individual efforts. The Health Village destination for him was not only about the functionality of the digital tool but a state-of-mind of feeling supported, equipped, trusted, and autonomous to get to the other side where his bike was waiting for him.

The second image from the CSC workshop was done as a pair, which was a request of the two storytellers. One of the storytellers was a neurologist and the other, a nurse. In this picture, they described the Health Village as something "positive," where practitioners are hard at work, and those who come to the village are welcomed and joyful. As the neurologist expressed herself: "We hope to bring health and, in this sense, the name [Health Village] has a positive echo" (workshop notes, 3.5.2019) (Fig. 5.5).

Differing from the picture in Fig. 5.4, the metaphor and the tool is contributing to a community of practitioners who are serving the village. The nurse and neurologists are working on the roof, while others benefit from their skills, motivation, and teamwork.

Fig. 5.4 An example of a metaphoric field interpretation

Fig. 5.5 An example of health care practitioners' interpretation of a metaphoric field

Part Four

The Material Story: Updating Scripts and the Report

From the initial contact with the workplace to the last moments together in the workshop, the Story Mediator takes detailed memos and notes, and through each stage, offloads these interpretations onto another Story Mediator.

In most respects, CSC has an ethnographic approach to research; however, it is developed from the original practice, which used video and audio recordings of all sessions and subsequent transcriptions. The original practice was influenced by traditional qualitative methods, and yet, in practice, storytellers gave feedback that recording took away from the intimacy of sharing with the Story Meditator.

With a work as craft mindset, we have decided that the practice of attentively listening, observing, and being present for the storyteller should be symbolically and materially respected with the sole use of a pad of paper and a pen. This allows the Story Mediator to listen but also embody their senses holistically in the workplace context.

Documenting the Collaborative Story Craft process is important for legitimacy and reliability of the tools, but also to hold the Story Mediators and the storytellers accountable.

In addition to the compromising zones and the areas of potential development witnessed in the workshop, documenting also adds another layer of validation to the exchange, ensuring that decision makers, as well as other contributors of the organisational change, can hold each other accountable going forward towards a common "destination."

"Gaslighting" is entrenched in power structures, and as organisational change in the workplace is initiated by the sense-giving of people in powerful positions, it is vital that the collective sensemaking process of Collaborative Storytelling is documented.

Gaslighting, a term now commonly used in various workplace contexts (e.g., for women of colour scientists, Rodrigues et al. 2021; in nurse academia, Christensen and Evans-Murray 2021), is understood as a form of psychological manipulation that aims to provoke self-doubt in the targeted individual or member of a targeted group, making the individual and/or group members question their own memory, perception, and sanity.

Gaslighting in the workplace can occur when individuals perform actions that cause colleagues to question themselves and their actions in a way that is detrimental to their careers (Adkins 2019).

The report serves as a material artefact that the process occurred, there was an effort to achieve purposeful consent, and that each member could share their lived experiences. As written by Hannah Ardent (1968, p. 105) in her book *Men in Dark Times* about twentieth century author Karen Christentze Dinesen, who wrote under the male pen name of Isak Dinesen:

> It is true that storytelling reveals meaning without committing the error of defining it, that it brings about consent and reconciliation with things as they really are, and that we may even trust it to contain eventually by implication that last word which we expect from "day of judgement." And yet, if we listen to Isak Dinesen's "philosophy" of storytelling and think of her life in the light of it, we cannot help becoming aware of how the slightest misunderstanding, the slightest shift of emphasis in the wrong direction, will inevitably ruin everything.

In light of Ardent's writing, the material story is not fixed, as it is ever-evolving and changing to different times and contexts. With a material story, there is possibility for growth, expansion, and continuous questioning of what is truth and purpose at the workplace. As Martin Luther King Jr. spoke in his 1968 speech: "Power properly understood is nothing but the ability to achieve purpose. It is the strength required to bring about social, political and economic change."

As storytellers, each participant of the CSC intervention possesses a crafted script that can be used for their chosen audience in the future.

After the CSC workshop, the entire documented process is materialised by the Story Mediators within three weeks following the last session of CSC. This document is sent to the individuals in positions of power as a material artefact of Collaborative Storytelling, representing a sensemaking process activity in organisational change. The document has the potential to garner consent, legitimacy, and inclusion to future sense-giving processes of change.

Conclusions

Collaborative Story Craft intervention initiates a process of awareness. This process not only calls attention to the hidden power of stories during organisational change but it also reveals how different individuals experience change through their embodied senses, taking into account the social worlds that they come from. Through CSC, it is possible to explore the hidden stories and understand how they influence our judgments or even govern our decisions.

Although the work with members of the organisation and their stories initiates with CSC, building narratives for collaboration in times of change can continue beyond the intervention, if Collaborative Storytelling Activity (CSA) is incorporated into organisational practices.

Through Story Mediation, acknowledging members of the organisation as storytellers and including their voices can enable everyone involved to communicate more effectively during new cycles of the organisation's story. Investing in Story Mediation training directed at practitioners that belong to the community of practice would ensure that the work as craft mindset can be used systematically for collaboration. In that sense, consulting with external Story Mediators would be a possibility but not a requirement. In our view, this would be a sustainable approach to build on the organisation's narratives during times of change and beyond.

Notes

1. This paradoxical realisation (of the Story Mediator having an audience), also acknowledges him/her as a storyteller and therefore as a contributor in the Collaborative Storytelling Activity of the organisation. Although Story Mediators are collaborators during the Collaborative Story Craft process, they do not seek credit in the public story, which is told by the members of the organisation.
2. We found that the circular model is a more accessible version for organisational members and easier to understand.
3. See Anderson and Jack (1998) for "learning to listen"; see Fromm (1998) for "the art of listening."

References

Adkins, Karen C. 2019. Gaslighting by crowd. *Social Philosophy Today* 35: 75–87.

Anderson, Kathryn, and Dana C. Jack. 1998. Learning to listen: Interview techniques and analyses. In *The oral history reader*, ed. Robert Perks and Alistair Thomson. New York: Routledge.

Arendt, Hannah. 1968. *Men in dark times*. Florida: Houghton Mifflin Harcourt.

Christensen, Martin, and Anne Evans-Murray. 2021. Gaslighting in nursing academia: A new or established covert form of bullying? *Nursing Forum* 56: 640–647.

Cleland Silva, T., and Paulo de Tarso Fonseca Silva. 2019. Validating change through collaborative story craft. In *SAGE research methods cases part 2 (SAGE research methods cases)*. Thousand Oaks: SAGE. https://doi.org/10.4135/9781526478245.

Cleland Silva, Tricia, and Paulo de Tarso Fonseca Silva. 2021. Collaborative Story Craft as a tool for inclusive workplace practices. In *History and storytelling in business*, ed. Albert Mills, Nick Deal, and David Boje. Singapore: World Scientific.

Fine, Gary Alan. 2003. Crafting authenticity: The validation of identity in self-taught art. *Theory and Society* 32: 153–180.

Fromm, Eric. 1998. *The art of listening*. New York: Continuum.

Jasanoff, Sheila. 2015. One. Future imperfect: Science, technology, and the imagination of modernity. In *Dreamscapes of modernity*, ed. Shelia Jasanoff and Sang-Hyun Kim, 1–33. Chicago: Chicago University Press.

Luckman, Susan. 2015. *Craft and the creative economy*. Switzerland: Springer.

Rodrigues, Michelle A., Ruby Mendenhall, and Kathryn B.H. Clancy. 2021. "There's realizing, and then there's realizing": How social support can counter

gaslighting of women of color scientists. *Journal of Women and Minorities in Science and Engineering* 27 (2): 1–23.
Sennett, Richard. 2008. *The craftsman*. London: Penguin.
Smith, Melanie, and László Puczkó. 2008. *Health and wellness tourism*. New York: Routledge.

CHAPTER 6

Crafting the Future Story Together

Abstract In this chapter, we discuss how after the Collaborative Story Craft intervention, practitioners can continue crafting and building their future stories together at work. Work engagement requests material resources and support, a sense of psychological and physical safety to be oneself, and meaningful rewards and recognition.

Although narratives and stories, on the surface, may seem fixed, raising awareness of the stories through Collaborative Storytelling provides an opportunity to create and maintain an organisational culture which strives for inclusion through responsible and sustainable practices of change.

Keywords Employee engagement • Metaphoric fields • Political and social activism • Sustainability • Story Craftivism

Life is a journey to be experienced, not a problem to be solved
—Winnie the Pooh, A.A. Milne

The presence of a Story Mediator is not a permanent fixture, just like Michael White's metaphor of scaffolding when working with stories in therapeutic practice. With this in mind, each stage of Collaborative Story Craft gives potential tools and skills to continue building narratives at

T. Cleland Silva, P. de Tarso Fonseca Silva, *Making Sense of Work Through Collaborative Storytelling*,
https://doi.org/10.1007/978-3-030-89446-7_6

work in various situations and times by the actors within the community of practice. Like Paulo Freire (1970), who empowered rural farmers with literacy skills needed for their life circumstances, Collaborative Story Craft strives to provide skills for future story exchange independently.

To continue building narratives towards sustainable and inclusive change requests a work as craft mindset to stay open, curious, and critical of the stories and metaphors exchanged at the workplace. This also means taking a moral stance and responsibility of what and how stories are exchanged and their material consequences on the work and individual well-being.

In 2017, a storyteller in a Collaborative Story Craft workshop mentioned to her colleagues that she was frustrated and tired of focusing on short-term production deadlines and not discussing the bigger vision behind the work's deeper purpose. To tell this story, she got up and drew a brick wall on a white board and described herself as a stick figure with an arrow starting from her chest. The arrow barely made it over the wall, and yet the other side of the wall is what she yearned for. She described this feeling as wanting something more from her work, to feel that her contribution mattered.
Similarly, work psychologist William Kahn (1990), inspired by the stories of summer camp counsellors, wrote that employees feel engaged at work when they have access and support to material resources, they feel physically and emotionally safe to be oneself, and the work is meaningful through recognition and rewards. In other words, their effort and contribution matters to the community of practice, and when it does not, they physically and psychologically withdraw from their working role.

Most often, a fast pace of production that is driven by short-term deadlines and profit-oriented goals leads to what André Spicer calls in his book "Business Bullshit" a "Sisyphus's to-do list" (2018, p. 69).

Sisyphus's story is similar to "hitting a wall" with meaningless work. In his case, Sisyphus was punished by the Greek God Hades for misdeeds in life by being condemned to the eternal task of rolling a large stone to the top of a hill, from which it always rolled down again.

Being in a constant state of rushing to get work done and not reflecting on the deeper purpose can lead to disengagement, emotional tax, burnout, and people leaving the workplace all together. It can also create a sense of "hopelessness" (see Cook 2007 on psychiatric nurses) or not seeing beyond the wall as to why the work matters.

Story Craftivism

As practitioners, when we talk about storytelling, it is common for people to signify story work as a "hobby" or project, their sensemaking of storytelling as something "trendy," and they treat it like a "buzzword."

Needless to say, there is nothing novel about telling stories, but perhaps a motive to strategically use stories as a means to a commodified, capitalist end (Boje 1995). Storytelling for inauthentic purposes is like constructing craft products and services as "handmade" for the sole purpose of appealing to conscious consumerism (Bell et al. 2019). Inauthentic storytelling and craft become more an instrument at the expense of connection and deeper collective meaning.

Nevertheless, there is hope. In our field of work, practitioners, who are passionate about stories and critical of dominant narratives, are growing as a community and their practices are increasingly more well defined. In this growing community, there is a sense of responsibility expressed through narratives of sustainable practices towards a bigger, collective purpose. This sense of responsibility is a common theme, which we identify in our peers and in ourselves.

The nuances of storytelling practices, which resonate with us, go beyond "business as usual" (Scheyvens et al. 2016), as they deal with and aspire for sustainable and inclusive change in working life and other global systems. These ways of working with stories can be described as social activism or what we call "Story Craftivism."

Story Craftivism is Collaborative Storytelling with a work as craft mindset. Story Craftivism is a movement that challenges dominant narratives and scripts to promote social and sustainable change through the exchange of authentic stories.

Like most forms of social activism, conscious raising and resistance derives from times of crisis, driven by meaningful motivations for individual and collective change.

As an intervention method, Collaborative Story Craft was built on four questions we asked ourselves in relation to equity and inclusion (Cleland Silva 2021):

1. What if the dominant collective story of a group did not resonate with all the members?
2. What if this disconnect was the cause (not the symptom) of tensions in the group?
3. Could we create a method that united the members under a common story or metaphor?
4. And could this common story lead to multiple voices and possible inclusion in the collective story?

The questions we posed many years ago came from our desire to make sense of our lived experiences as "foreigners" working and living in a Nordic welfare state. Both of us are socially constructed as "highly skilled immigrants" based on our nationalities and acquired education, which affects how we navigate and experience the local system of governance influenced by our social and global rank. For instance, local narratives constructed about "foreigners" impacted how we navigated and made sense of our physical and social lives as well as our economic opportunities to acquire either education skills and/or work while raising a family. At this time, our sense of community held many members who also identified as "foreigners" and yet each person had different material experiences based on how their social identities were constructed by the local narratives (see Cleland Silva 2019, pp. 80–81). We can only explain this "foreigner" sensemaking of embodied lived experiences as stepping in and out of dominant and peripheral worlds and, at times, this discomfort of the unknown or being perceived as the unknown could feel like purgatory. Yet, through these circumstances, we saw humanity in others, ourselves, and in the arbitrariness of seemingly fixed narratives and practices. In many respects, honouring our stories and others helped us get through the hard times and craft stories that are more resilient, emphatic, and accountable.

The strangers in your midst shall be to you as the native born, for you know the stranger's heart, for you were strangers in the land of Egypt.
Exodus 23:9

As a metaphoric field, purgatory can be a state of mind that is manifested in different scales in different social worlds, where power dynamics can stir one's faith subjectively and unpredictably. People who are dependent on inclusion find themselves in a situation where being included becomes a condition for having access to resources and opportunities. Those people are likely the same ones whose stories are silenced or do not relate to the stories of the dominant group.

Expanding on the meaning of being "foreigners," we consider the opposite sides of power. One side controls what stories should be told, while the other side expects to be "included" in a story where they are seen and heard. Both sides cannot exist alone, and yet there are hidden conditions and responsibilities associated with the equilibrium of stories.

"Foreigner" to us is anyone who seeks to be part of something bigger but is still uniquely different. The dominant story at work is one of the social worlds where "foreignness" is at play, as our embodied stories are either included or dismissed. That description is a reminder that anyone could be a foreigner, standing at the peripheral borders of a bigger powerful story.

In order to craft a future story together, we need to understand our position of power without neglecting our responsibilities. This begs the questions: What is your type of "foreignness"? Where do you position yourself? Do you often feel like a foreigner? If so, can you enter the bigger story? If you see yourself in the bigger story, how do you see the walls? What do you see through the windows? Can you open any doors?

Conclusions

In Chap. 2, we introduced the Social Worlds of Snakes and Ladders to illustrate how power is evasive and interwoven in systems of narratives where dominant, social narratives are context-specific, relational, and most often, considered fixed.

In this chapter, through the Story Craftivist lens, we described our own experiences as "foreigners," and how, through these experiences, we navigated different circumstances which were influenced by our perceived social ranks in context.

Entering the unknown and being perceived as the unknown strengthened our sense of personal power. It also cultivated our self-awareness of the impact of dominant narratives on the material and social worlds of those constructed.

When personal power is activated, it can also be synchronised with others to question well-established stories, not with the intention of replacing the stories of those in power, but to consider an exchange of stories from different positions and lived experiences. When this approach is incorporated in organisational change, Collaborative Storytelling Activity will no longer be a parallel activity to the work, but rather integrated into the activity system through ethical and sustainable practices.

References

Bell, Emma, Gianluigi Mangia, Scott Taylor, and Maria Laura Toraldo, eds. 2019. *The organization of craft work: Identities, meanings, and materiality.* New York: Routledge.

Boje, D.M. 1995. Stories of the storytelling organization: A postmodern analysis of Disney as "Tamara-Land". *Academy of Management Journal* 38 (4): 997–1035.

Cleland Silva, Tricia. 2019. *Translational management and globalised workers: Nurses beyond human resources.* New York: Routledge.

———. 2021. Meaningful and inclusive workplaces through story. *TedxMetropolia University*, April 22. https://www.ted.com/talks/tricia_cleland_silva_meaningful_and_inclusive_workplaces_through_story.

Cook, Gina M. 2007. Burnout and Hopelessness among nurses working on Midwest Community psychiatric hospital units. *Theses and Dissertations*: 3171.

Freire, Paulo. 1970. *Pedagogy of the oppressed.* New York: Continuum.

Kahn, William A. 1990. Psychological conditions of personal engagement and disengagement at work. *Academy of Management Journal* 33 (4): 692–724.

Scheyvens, Regina, Glenn Banks, and Emma Hughes. 2016. The private sector and the SDGs: The need to move beyond 'business as usual'. *Sustainable Development* 24 (6): 371–382.

Spicer, André. 2018. *Business bullshit.* New York: Routledge.

CHAPTER 7

Approaching Work Stories with a Craft Mindset

Abstract This chapter starts with a metaphorical story called "Building a Health Village." The story was created by the first author and is based on empirical data collected between 2018 and 2019. The data was acquired through formal interviews and two Collaborative Story Craft workshops with health care practitioners and other stakeholders co-creating a digital service platform. The story also draws from informal conversations told to the first author over a period of 15 years in a Nordic welfare state. During this time, she has navigated various social worlds as an immigrant, student, cleaner, teacher, academic researcher, business co-founder, and parent. Both authors applied their work as craft mindset to build questions for those interpreting the story.

The aim of the chapter is to emphasise that stories and narrations change and transform as individuals continuously make sense of their social and material surroundings. Stories are also free floating as they narrate events to different audiences. Like sensemaking and craftwork, narrating and telling stories to make sense of embodied lived experiences never ends or stops cleanly. Rather, stories enter new cycles of purpose and possibilities from different positions, depending on the context and the audience.

Keywords Community of practice • Digitalisation • Equity • Health care • Inclusion • Narratives • Organisational change • Sociomaterial practices • Stories

T. Cleland Silva, P. de Tarso Fonseca Silva, *Making Sense of Work Through Collaborative Storytelling*,
https://doi.org/10.1007/978-3-030-89446-7_7

It's the simple things in your life that make up the bulk of it.
The mundane is where we live and we end up missing most of it.
We find it again in the silence and in attention of everyday life.
—Eric Overby, Poet and Surgical Technologist

A Story: Building a Health Village

It all started with wanting to help people who felt alone.

"How do we reach them before it's too late?" The head Psychiatrist, Henry, asked his silent colleagues, John and Maria, who were captivated by the question as they also had the same concern.

"If we could create a place to receive our patients that was easy to access. Not a confusing maze of administration and scattered information from many sources. A place where they felt safe, where we could address their individual needs without them having to come to the hospital." Henry pauses and looks out the window of the staff coffee room. "We have lost so many people because they don't know how to connect with us."

John replied pensively, "Yeah, a place where they felt welcomed and wanted like a village, where everyone knows each other. In the small village I grew up in, everyone helped each other. Once, we had a huge snowstorm that blew out the electricity for days, and even though the temperatures were fatal, no one died, as neighbours checked on neighbours. The local community centre provided beds and hot meals, especially to the elderly living alone. This happened years ago, and people still talk about it."

The psychiatrists work at the largest public hospital in a small Nordic country. The hospital has over 30 specialised medicine departments. All the health care practitioners would agree that the hospital is a great place to work. The practitioners are encouraged to work autonomously, together with the support of their managers. Rooted in Nordic social egalitarian values, the practitioners would expect nothing less for themselves and their fellow citizens. Everyone has a right to good quality care and fair work with integrity.

With John and Maria's encouragement, Henry pursued approval from his boss and applied for funding at the hospital to create a digital platform that has information on mental health services and a simple booking system for online therapy. The funding was approved on the condition that if the pilot worked, other specialised medicines could also contribute with their own practice.

(*continued*)

(continued)

Two years later, the digital health village was opened with over 32 specialised medicine houses. Like pioneers, the practitioners built the village through common values and beliefs of a hoped-for future, and their collective tacit knowledge of the past. To ensure the village houses would cater to the needs of the community, the practitioners invite and encourage individuals who use the service to consult on the design and practices of the houses. The feedback is continuous through conversations between the practitioners involved in the build and the community it serves.

One beautiful morning, John, Maria, and Henry were in the staff coffee room again, deep in conversation. There were other staff members, a few nurses, and secretaries, who joined as they reminisced about how far the health village had come.

"It feels so much easier to connect with the community. I feel great about my work and can really see first-hand how it is impacting people's well-being," John says with a smile.

Jenny, a secretary, nods: "I have worked here for over 30 years and have never been asked by a doctor or a practitioner what my thoughts are on the needs of our community and how to serve them better. Since the health village, I have helped with digital content, and I have a deep sense of ownership of the village that I proudly introduce to anyone who asks or listens!" She laughs.

Henry looks at Jenny in astonished guilt and thinks, "I never thought to ask Jenny her opinion, I just thought we did such different work. Don't we? She did have a great idea the other day about short videos explaining the symptoms of burnout. I wonder if she ever experienced that here? I know I have."

Petra, a nurse manager, brings up what she is working on, "We just finished a page on loneliness amongst the elderly living in our city. Talking about it with the other nurses and the social workers has been such an eye-opener. When we are so focused on getting the work done here at the hospital, we forget that the people we don't see still need our care. Many don't have families and asking them about their stories has made me think of my own sense of community. Like yesterday, I talked to Margaret, my 80-year-old neighbour, for a bit longer in the yard. I say hi to her, but usually, I rush by because of work or errands. I felt calm and my spirits lifted after our conversation. I look forward to talking to her again."

****

In order to get into a work as craft mindset, we propose a set of questions in different parts of the story. To start, consider the following:

- Who are the actors?
- Is there a dominant narrative? If so, by whom?
- What is the call for action?
- How many stories or social worlds do you identify?
- Are there predominant metaphors? Do they mean anything specific to you?
- What is the overall feeling from the interactions?

Close to the hospital, Susan sits in her small apartment that she shares with two other nurses. She's scheduled for work in a few hours and asked some of her friends for a quick visit.

Susan has been feeling sad lately. When she came to this country five years ago, she was excited and hopeful. She had worked hard for her nursing degree in the Philippines and was grateful for all the work experience she achieved as a psychiatric ICU nurse.

When she was recruited, her plans were to continue developing her skills with a larger salary, meet new people, and maybe travel. She loves being a nurse, and she knows she is good at her job.

She lets out a sigh and gets up to boil water for their tea. She tells herself that the tea and a quick chat with friends will make her feel more herself, maybe even rested. She hasn't been sleeping well lately as the shifts at the hospital have been long and difficult, and she continues most of her working days studying to certify her previous degree and practice the local language. She also thinks about her feelings of disappointment which keep her awake wondering and worrying.

"What an irony that you care for others who have insomnia and anxiety. They had much bigger issues than you, and now you feel sorry for yourself! You should feel lucky to have a job in such a safe place!" Susan chides herself aloud.

There is a loud knock on the door. "Coming!" Susan yells and laughs at how loud Julie always knocks as if Susan didn't know she was coming. Susan and Julie text message each other easily 10 times a day.

Julie and Rick tumble in. Julie is the same age as Susan, mid-30s, and Rick is in his late 40s. Both are great nurses; both are fantastic parents. Rick's children are teenagers, whereas Julie's are still in day care. Julie

(*continued*)

(continued)

and Rick moved from the Philippines about a decade ago and studied their previous degree again to work as nurses. They struggled with the language at first, but now they are citizens after proving their command.

"You look terrible!" Julie teases but is concerned. Susan has said she is not feeling herself lately and that she has been missing "her family back home."

"Yeah, I know. I think I am burnt out. All these long shifts and having to study nursing again while working. It is just too much! I don't have anyone to speak to about this at work as I am either alone on my shift or we are too busy," she pauses. "I know I should get some help or talk to someone about getting more down time, but I always feel overwhelmed with asking. Who do I ask? And to be honest, I am afraid they are going to blame me for feeling this way. Like, I should be grateful to have what I have and just suck it up until it feels normal."

"That is ridiculous, Susan, and you know it!" Rick interjects. "I have been here for a long time, and I can tell you that it doesn't get better. I always feel like my language is not good enough or I need to prove myself more at work so they can finally give me work that I deserve. But it never comes! You got to take care of yourself."

Julie puts her arm around Susan. Julie also felt frustrated with her skills not being used. She has also felt lonely at work. Like the other day, she was sitting in the staff coffee room, and everyone was talking loudly about this health village. She had heard about creating online services and wanted to get involved, but her manager never asked her. Was she supposed to ask? Would they give her working time? She is a whiz on social media with many following her blog about being a nurse abroad.

****

Before continuing with the story, think about the following questions:

- Who are the actors?
- Is there a common theme?
- Is there a problem that should be addressed?
- Consider the metaphorical social world of Snakes and Ladders in Chap. 2. How does this part of the story compare to the previous one?
- What is the overall feeling from the interactions?

Later that day, Susan is sitting in a meeting at work, her manager, Petra, is explaining how successful the health village has become. Most of the nurses present are animated and sharing their own experiences about how the village is inclusive. Petra says, "I feel it may have saved many lives."

This is great! Susan thinks as she looks at the platform which is projected on the screen. But looking at all the images and reading the descriptions of the services, she hesitates. These services are great, but why am I still confused? Where do I get the information I need? And why am I only hearing about this now? Why haven't I been asked to participate? There is so much I have to say!

That evening, Susan could not sleep. She knew she had to get up early for work, but no matter how hard she tried, she couldn't shake the feeling of loneliness. "Maybe this was a mistake, and I shouldn't have left home. I am a good nurse, but I don't know what they want from me here. Do they need me or am I just another nurse?" She adjusted her body by throwing her leg over a pillow. Her back and shoulders hurt, and she was frightened about not caring for herself. A little past 2 a.m., her body finally succumbed to sleep.

****

Take a moment to breathe and think about the story*:*

- Do you identify a connection between different social worlds?
- What do you think the overall theme of the story will be?
- Is there an actor who stands out for you? Why?

In the morning, Susan arrived a few minutes before her shift. She liked starting with coffee in the staff room and socialising before her rounds. As she prepared the coffee, her manager, Petra, walked in.

"Good morning, Susan. How are you?" Petra asks while grabbing a clean mug from the dishwasher and heading towards Susan who's brewing coffee.

"I am fine, but tired. I haven't been sleeping lately." Susan responds with a warm smile.

Petra smirks "Yeah, I hear ya! I didn't sleep well either, guess it comes with being a nurse working shifts."

(*continued*)

(continued)

Susan hesitates but decides to speak, "Actually, I like being a nurse and shifts don't bother me. Sure, the heavy lifting is hard on my body, but I love connecting with people, and I'm passionate about mental health." She pauses. "Lately, I have been wondering if I am doing enough here at the hospital. I feel like I have so much to share, but I am not sure who I should ask about taking on more responsibility."

Petra listens intently but adds only a few words of comfort with no direct suggestions, "I am sorry to hear that, we know you are great at your job."

A few moments of silence is broken when Susan asks to pour coffee for Petra. They fill their mugs and move together to sit at the table.

"You know, when I was a kid, I never had problems with sleeping because my family had this nightly ritual of sharing stories about the day," Susan explains. "My parents would tuck me and my brother into bed, and we would take turns sharing what happened that day. Of course, there were good and bad days, but even on the bad days, just by sharing, I could relax to peacefully fall asleep."

Petra nods, "That sounds a bit like sauna with my kids. On Saturday nights, we all go to sauna to relax and connect after a busy week of work and school. My kids tell some amazing stories, and it is such a pleasure to really see and hear them being animated about friends and experiences."

As they sip their coffee and continue talking, Henry arrives, grateful to see a full pot of coffee. He grabs a cup, which he fills to the brim with his favourite morning drink and joins the women at the table.

"Good morning, Susan. Good morning, Petra."

"Good morning," both women warmly respond.

"Petra, by the way, when is the health village meeting today? Are all the nurses coming?" Henry asks.

"It's at 10 in room 303. I think everyone confirmed over our group email, so yeah, all will be there."

Susan blushes and thinks, "Group email? Why wasn't I included?"

Henry speaks with enthusiasm, "I am so pleased with how well we are building this health village. Can you believe that the idea came from this very room a few years ago?! We have made such progress, and it really is improving how the patients get good, quality care."

(*continued*)

(continued)

Susan turns and asks Henry, "Where did the idea of the health village come from?"

Henry shares, "Well, we wanted to help people to not feel alone by connecting with us with more ease. Having our services online creates the feeling of a small community like a village where people know where to find us and get the help they deserve."

Susan recalled her recent experience of looking at the website in the group meeting. She most definitely did not feel that she belonged in that village.

Susan asks a few more questions, "Why only one language? Are there plans to make the information available in English? Not everyone who needs help can understand or make sense of what support is possible in the health village."

Petra looks at Henry and then back at Susan, "You are right, I never thought of that. I was mostly thinking about my regular patients, my elderly neighbour, and to be honest, myself," Petra responds and asks, "Susan, are you coming to today's meeting?"

"I wasn't part of the group email, but yes, I would like to join. Thanks for asking," Susan responded.

"Well, time to get started," Henry says while standing up. Petra joins him to wash her mug, and they walk out of the coffee room together.

Susan stays behind to finish her coffee. She thinks, "I wonder if Petra can add me to the group email? Should I ask if we will get support and time to work on the village? What about the other nurses? How does it affect their work?"

She stands to wash her mug, and before leaving the room, she quickly sends a WhatsApp message to Rick and Julie, "Guess who got invited to the health village!"

Susan switches her mobile to silent and places it gently into her pocket. A surge of energy runs through her body as she walks quickly out the door. "I am definitely gonna get Julie to join," she thinks determinedly.

Building on the Previous Narratives:

- What is this story about? Are there main themes or metaphors?
- Is there a protagonist?
- What is the main activity?

- What is the object of work?
- Are there communication tools?
- Are there rules?
- Who are the decision makers?
- Who belongs to the community of practice?
- Is there collaboration?
- Are the responsibilities well defined?
- Which voices are included or excluded from building on the narratives?
- What is the overall level of occupational well-being?
- Can other wellness dimensions be identified in the story?
- How do they differ among the actors?

Consider Yourself a Decision Maker*:*

- Which changes should take place? How?

Consider Yourself a Story Mediator*:*

- Which stories should be mediated? Which themes intersect? Which combination of actors should meet to exchange stories and why?

We read the story "Building a Health Village" to various audiences, including our 10-year-old daughter, who was up in arms about how poorly Susan was treated by the other health care practitioners. Others felt that Susan was too optimistic in the end and should have been more critical and assertive about the exclusive practices of a health village that promoted inclusion. One person remarked, "if I was left out of group emails, that would be enough for me to leave!" And yet, this is the crux of the story based on data collected over 15 years: your position of power and how you make sense of and act on your experiences are social, embodied, contextual, and purpose-driven. Susan did not choose to be excluded from engaging with her work. Rather how the health village, as a digital tool, was socially constructed and subsequently practised was influenced by the dominant social narratives which afforded meaning and significance to the health village metaphor. Susan's exclusion was not driven by her lack of motivation, curiosity, and willingness, but rather a lack of an opportunity to discuss her unique experiences in the community of practice. In other words, she is excluded from an opportunity to collaborate and create a metaphorical story based on collective sensemaking of the health village.

In social and material worlds, power is always present, but difficult to identify and communicate. Most often, like in the case of Susan, making sense of the psychological and physical effects of power happens through communication but also painful symptoms within the body. Sense-making is a retrospective and prospective process which never stops and starts cleanly (Weick 1995). People have an inherent need to continuously make sense of what is happening (Wright and Manning 2004, p. 638) through feedback loops (Argyris and Schön 1974) in relation to social interactions, bodily experiences, and the material environment (Sandberg and Tsoukas 2020). Small mundane acts like Susan boiling water for tea while waiting for trusted friends or sharing coffee in the staff room with colleagues may seem insignificant, and yet, these very situations provide her continuous feedback as to how she is positioned within the cultural-historical context in relation to others and to her purpose being there.

Because social and embodied lived experiences are individually unique, most often it is the individual who feels responsible for material and social consequences of the exclusion. Stories like Susan's are more common as practitioners navigate social worlds based on global and local narratives and from positions of ranked hierarchy that are beyond one's control. To build sustainable narratives in organisational change, members need to sense their own power and be open to understand how their power is perceived by others. As American novelist Alice Walker, said, "the most common way people give up their power is by thinking they don't have any" (quoted in Diamond 2016, p. 169).

To bring about effective, responsible, and inclusive change at the workplace requires leaders (or the dominant sense givers) to "impact and influence situations across diverse and unpredictable contexts, legitimately (with implied or explicit cooperation and agreement of others), for the greater good" (Diamond 2016, p. 196). In a nutshell, it is about listening and making sense of stories; and when there is a recurring metaphor like the health village, questioning what the metaphor means to those affected in practice. Deep reflections of how and why narratives and metaphors are used and of the subsequent effects in sensemaking can reveal deeper meaning of taken-for-granted practices such as who is included and excluded in a group email related to, for instance, a new tool for doing the work.

Introducing new tools to the workplace like a digital platform such as the health village can give practitioners an opportunity to reinvent their ways of working (Nicolini 2011) and harness lively discussions about the tools' purpose. Stories about the tools, which construct the tools' instrumentality and potential use, are "free floating" in space and time from a formal meeting or group email to having coffee in the staff room. With a work as craft mindset, new tools can ignite curiosity to tinker with the possibilities of what could be by drawing from a community of practice based on shared skills, purpose, and traditions.

The story of the health village started with a perceived "good intention": to help those who felt lonely by providing accessible and good quality care. Nonetheless, by developing and practicing the tool within the boundaries of the dominant social world's identities and narratives, the tool became a material extension of the dominant group's sensegiving.Taking stock of the sensemaking processes, the central and critical question that arises is what is the metaphorical story of the health village *about*? By asking this question in relation to the work and its shared purpose within a community of practice, the question then expands to other questions like:

- What is loneliness?
- What is a village?
- What is health?
- What is the purpose of a health village?
- Who are the members of a health village?
- Who is a part of the health village community?
- Who comes to the health village for help? Are they a part or separate from the community in the village?
- What happens in a health village?
- What are the rules in the health village?
- What is the future of the health village?

Essential to making sense of the recurring metaphors at work is not questioning others, but rather being interested (Terkel and Parker 1998, p.126) and being open to sharing stories from one's social and occupational position. Collaborative Storytelling with a work as craft mindset provides the possibility of actively listening with curiosity and motivation, to hold the space for another storyteller, while exchanging one's own story by engaging with the metaphor. In the case of the health village, the health care workers and other stakeholders constructing a village to provide accessible, good quality health care services for those who are lonely is the metaphorical story. With a Story Mediator, the externalisation and validation of each member's story in relation to the work and the metaphor accords the members an opportunity to craft their stories in relation to the shared purpose of building an accessible and inclusive health village. Recurring themes of the storytellers are loneliness, a sense of community and belonging, and helping others feel included and provided with accessible, good quality care.

From the crafted scripts of their own stories, each member in the Collaborative Story Craft workshop can participate and give consent to what the metaphor means and how it impacts their sensemaking of the work and the organisational change. The Story Mediators can open the discussions to the storytellers' social and embodied lived experiences in relation to the metaphor without the dominating members imposing assumptions for the community of practice as a whole.

Conclusions

The story portrayed in this chapter was not a direct report of a real series of events; however, it is based on interviews and workshops from previous research. As such, it carries many elements of reality with similar material consequences and outcomes on those involved. Often, organisational change is messy, confusing, non-inclusive, and does not comply with a clear end. Crafting a story that illustrates the challenges of communities of practice can support the externalisation of stories and the exchange of ideas to craft a common future story together.

Approaching work stories with a craft mindset instigates the members of communities of practice to have a problem-solving perspective on collaborative practices. Decision makers, who value inclusiveness as an important component for sustainable change, will question which stories build on the interests of the collective. By imagining questions to the challenges faced in an organisational story will enable the work as craft mindset to be activated. The questions should consider empathy and a well-defined system of values that speaks to the organisational members. If a system of values is not clear or codes of conduct are not well defined, they also should be put into question.

In our practice, the work as craft mindset is influenced by a combination of models,[1] theories,[2] methodologies,[3] and values[4] that interplay with creativity, intuition, embodied senses, embodied lived experiences, and sensemaking ability. We question dominant narratives, recurring themes, and metaphors, trusting that the affordance given to a story, a system of stories, or process of change depends on inclusion and the interaction of different actors that belong to the Collaborative Storytelling Activity System of a community of practice.

Notes

1. For example, CSC models represented in Figs. 3.1, 3.2, and 3.3.
2. Cultural Historical Activity Theory (CHAT), Collaborative Storytelling Activity system (CSA).
3. Story Mediation and Collaborative Story Craft intervention.
4. TILES.

References

Argyris, Chris, and Donald Schön. 1974. *Theory in practice: Increasing professional effectiveness*. Madison: Jossey-bass.

Diamond, Julie. 2016. *Power: A user's guide*. New Mexico: Belly Song Press.

Nicolini, Davide. 2011. Practice as the site of knowing: Insights from the field of telemedicine. *Organization Science* 22: 602–620.

Sandberg, Jörgen, and Haridimos Tsoukas. 2020. Sensemaking reconsidered: Towards a broader understanding through phenomenology. *Organization Theory* 1: 1–31. https://doi.org/10.1177/2631787719879937.

Terkel, Studs, and Tony Parker. 1998. Interviewing the interviewer. In *The oral history reader*, ed. Robert Perks and Alistair Thomson, 123–128. New York: Routledge.

Weick, Karl E. 1995. *Sensemaking in organizations*. Thousand Oaks: SAGE.

Wright, Charles R., and Michael R. Manning. 2004. Resourceful sensemaking in an administrative group. *Journal of Management Studies* 41: 623–643.

CHAPTER 8

Conclusions

Abstract This chapter closes with the acknowledgement of mentors and the hero/heroine within us. With a work as craft mindset, Collaborative Storytelling seeks to frame individual stories within wider, intertwined systems of narratives. The opportunity to craft one's story is possible for all of us individually. And yet, for collective change to happen, an exchange of stories of all those invested can ignite a mosaic of heroes and mentors that is not reliant on a single hero's story.

Collaborative Storytelling brings in a different type of power that benefits a wider system of narratives. Collective power is not only shared, it is multiplied.

Keywords Hero's Journey • Joseph Campbell • Mentors • Mentorship Mosaic • Story Craftivism • Sustainability • System of narratives

Art begins with craft, and there is no art until craft has been mastered
—Anthony Burgess

Over a decade ago, when we first started working with stories, we were not sure what we were doing, but intuitively knew that we were on the right path.

T. Cleland Silva, P. de Tarso Fonseca Silva, *Making Sense of Work Through Collaborative Storytelling*,
https://doi.org/10.1007/978-3-030-89446-7_8

"What do you mean you work with stories?" has been a frequent question asked, and to be fair, there were times where we felt that this question was asked in all aspects of our lives: at work, social gatherings, and most often in our home.

Although, at times, this question felt frustrating and exhausting, we are grateful to those who asked because it activated our own storytelling about what our purpose is, who we serve, and how we do our work.

It is now clear that we are tinkers and thinkers who are Story Craftivists. What this means in practice is to acknowledge and nurture authentic stories, striving to work for sustainable, inclusive change for individuals and communities. It is also about holding space and witnessing people make sense of their social and material worlds without judgement or giving advice on how their sensemaking should lead to their purpose.

Working with stories activates our minds, bodies, and hearts, and when we are "in the zone," we are transported into the imaginary landscape of the storyteller. Most often the catalyst into the zone are metaphors and stories where the individual creatively uses voice and their bodies (with any form of art expression) to explain how the story makes them feel while recalling an event, describing their experience, or imagining a situation.

As an audience, this experience is like being pulled by an invisible force that unites two worlds, and this is why we gave ourselves the title of Story Mediators to give words to "being in the middle" of the implicit and explicit, conscious or unconscious, the dominant and peripheral, and the material or symbolic worlds of embodied sensemaking and cognition.

Mentorship Mosaic

It is clear that our work with individual and organisational storytelling was preceded by other scholars and practitioners whose theorisation and methods informed and impacted Collaborative Storytelling, Story Mediation, and Collaborative Story Craft. Scholars such as David Boje and his work on antenarrative (2011), organisational storytelling practices in a Quantum Age (Boje 2008) and his collaboration with Kenneth Jørgensen on "True Storytelling" for sustainable problem-based learning (Jørgensen and Boje 2020). Yannis Gabriel's work on myths, archetypes, and fantasy in organisation and workplace narratives from a psychotherapist lens (1995, 2004) and Wendelin Küpers, Saku Mantere, and Matt Statler's work on strategy as storytelling.

Story Mediation and Collaborative Story Craft as a method was also cultivated when Paulo was a student at the Center for Research on Activity, Development and Learning (CRADLE), a hub for academics and practitioners established by Yrjö Engeström at the University of Helsinki. As well as Adele Clarke's method "Situational Analysis: grounded theory after the interpretive turn" (2005, Clarke et al. 2017) which influenced Tricia's positioning. Clarke's method is also an extension and deep appreciation to Anslem Strauss, a well-known grounded theorist on social worlds. Her work both honours her mentor's contribution but also shifts the paradigm of grounded theory to encapsulate interpretivism and Foucaultian discourse analysis of narrative, historical, and visual materials.

With a work as craft mindset, we aimed in this book not only to appreciate those that we have elected as our mentors, but also to make our own unique contribution to storytelling as a way to build narratives during organisational change. As written by Henry Mintzberg, theory and methods should be surprising, and this is the whole purpose of scientific contribution (2017, p. 10):

> Theory is insightful when it surprises, when it allows us to see profoundly, imaginatively, unconventionally into phenomena we thought we understood... (A professor of mine once said that theories go through three stages: first they're wrong; then they're subversive; finally they're obvious.)

Perhaps, this book is in the "subversive stage," and we are content with this defiance as we continue to break apart, question, stay curious, and sometimes struggle about what we say and do while taking ownership of our work with purpose, accountability, and self-awareness of the cultural-historical context. As Rollo May, an existential psychologist, once wrote in "The Courage to Create" (1975, p. 8):

> When I use the word rebel for the artist, I do not refer to revolutionary or to such things as taking over the dean's office; that is a different matter. Artists are generally soft-spoken persons who are concerned with their inner visions and images. But that is precisely what makes them feared by any coercive society. For they are the bearers of the human being's age-old capacity to be insurgent.

Through this collaborative journey as storytelling practitioners, we discovered that there are no such things as one theory, method, perspective, narration, or story. In fact, this essentialism leads to dubious explanations and destructive practices that isolate individuals or dominant groups and "hardens" creativity, innovation, and the possibilities for change. No one benefits from this narrow view of possibilities, especially those protecting it at any cost.

> The centipede was happy quite
> Until a toad in fun
> Said, "Pray, which leg goes after which?"
> That worked her mind to such a pitch,
> She lay distracted in a ditch
> Considering how to run.
> (Mrs. Edward Craster 1871; quoted by Mintzberg 2017)

Metaphors and storytelling invoke curiosity, being present, and actively listening, especially when they come through authentic narration. Metaphors and stories can provide courage and perseverance during uncertainty, times of difficulty, and entering the unknown.

In Joseph Campbell's 1949 book "The Hero of a thousand faces" (2008), he describes a pattern called the Hero's Journey based on his research of archetypes, myths, and stories from various cultures in the world.

The Hero's Journey is a metaphor-archetype where the hero leaves the comfort of the status quo because of a call to action. There are several stages that Campbell uses to describe venturing into the supernatural unknown where the hero encounters a mentor who guides the hero through obstacles. The hero triumphs victoriously before coming back from this mysterious adventure with powers to bestow onto his community.

Within this metaphor-archetype, we found that the hero and the mentor being singular felt limiting and isolating, especially when it comes to Collaborative Storytelling. As Rebecca Solnit wrote in her article "When the Hero is the problem", we can find strength in numbers rather than giving over our powers to one individual, endowed with the responsibility to protect the status quo.

She writes about the possibilities of collective action for positive social change which comes from people connecting more deeply to others rather than rising above them (April 2nd, 2019):

> ...that's what we get, over and over, and in the course of getting them [heroes] we don't get much of a picture of how change happens and what our role in it might be, or how ordinary people matter. "Unhappy the land that needs heroes" is a line of Bertold Brecht's I've gone to dozens of times, but now I'm more inclined to think, pity the land that thinks it needs a hero, or doesn't know it has lots and what they look like.

Questioning the hero as central to the story and inviting others to share their experiences in the story helps address "wicked problems" (Rittel and Webber 1973) like global inequity, climate change, and political divisiveness that affects all aspects of society, including the workplace. Collective problems and sustainable change can only be created and acted upon collectively.

We broke the hero and mentor mould by crafting the concept "Mentorship Mosaic." Mentorship Mosaic is the process of drawing from various lived experiences where a mentor, human and non-human, was encountered to help make meaningful sense, retrospectively, of events based on one's identity, social relationships, and cultural-historical context. This means that a mentor does not always narrate advice or support. A lesson does not need to be delivered directly from a mentor figure as it can be formed from feelings invoked by a process, such as reading a book of an author you will never meet in an old historical library.

To build Mentorship Mosaic is to acknowledge that although we live in a story, we do not encounter one single mentor for the whole journey. Every mentor is a master of his or her own craft, and it would be unrealistic and even unfair to expect that our mentors would be responsible to be a reference to our unique embodied experiences throughout all the cycles of our journey.

As we build on Joseph Campbell's work, we consider the Hero's and Heroine's journey as interdependent cycles within our own life story. This reminds us that for each cycle we have encountered different mentors. The lessons acquired from those mentors were not only timely and contextual, but they were directed at particular areas that needed to be developed in the hero within us.

Through Metaphorical Tourism, we can revisit those past cycles and reconnect with the stories that made a person, an event, or an entity become a mentor. This process validates the lessons and honours the mentors. And yet, revisiting past cycles also identifies the area in which the mentor could help us. That area is one tile to the Mentorship Mosaic that we, as heroes of our own story, are building throughout the cycles of our journey. To those of us who have had the opportunity to build a relationship with "human mentors", building a Mentorship Mosaic also allows us to identify the humanity in them. This craft mindset also releases our past mentors from being a reference point to all areas and phases of our story.

To craft a Mentorship Mosaic is to be able to see the lessons and stories that we have embodied and by doing that, making sense of how we can mentor ourselves and others.

Crafting Stories Through Empathy and Collective Courage

When we engage with Collaborative Storytelling, we have an exercise which we frequently use to get to know a new group. This exercise is called "sharing the ice cream" as a way to sweeten the common metaphor of "breaking the ice". This exercise consists of four simple questions:

My name is…
I am more than (primary identity seen by others). I am also…
My expectation for today is…
If I could choose a superpower, it would be…

We shared this exercise at the end of the book as an invitation: to consider a craft mindset of tinker and thinker, to become a mindful storyteller and maybe a Story Craftivist. Think about your responses. Where do they take you? Do they nurture the roots of your authentic story? Do they connect with your lifestyle and sense of responsibility in the world? Or do they take you in a Metaphorical Tourism to the future that you aspire to witness? As our paths have crossed, this exercise is also a reminder that this is just a continuation of a story and the beginning of a new cycle.

References and Suggested Further Readings

Arthur, Mary Alice. 2020. *365 Alive! Find your voice. Claim your story. Live your brilliant life*. Ohio: Firelight Publications.

Babb, Sanora. 2004. *Whose names are unknown*. Oklahoma: University of Oklahoma Press.

Boje, David M. 2008. *Storytelling organizational practices in a quantum age*. New York: Routledge.

———. 2011. *Storytelling and the future of organizations: An antenarrative handbook*. Edited by David Boje. New York: Routledge.
Campbell, Joseph. 2008. *The hero with a thousand faces (Collected works of Joseph Campbell)*. San Francisco: New World Library.
Clarke, Adele. 2005. *Situational analysis: Grounded theory after the Postmodern turn*. Thousand Oaks: Sage.
Clarke, Adele E., Carrie Friese, and Rachel S. Washburn. 2017. *Situational analysis: Grounded theory after the interpretive turn*. Thousand Oaks: Sage Publications.
Gabriel, Yiannis. 1995. The unmanaged organization: Stories, fantasies and subjectivity. *Organization studies* 16 (3): 477–501.
Gabriel, Yiannis. 2004. Narratives, stories and texts. *The Sage handbook of organizational discourse*. Newbury Park: SAGE publishing.
Heracleous, Loizos, and Claus D. Jacobs. 2008. *Crafting strategy: Embodied metaphors in practice*. Cambridge: Cambridge University Press.
Jørgensen, Kenneth M., and M. David Boje. 2020. Storytelling sustainability in problem based learning. In *Populism in higher education curriculum development*, ed. Romeo V. Turcan and John E. Reilly. London: Palgrave Macmillan.
King, Steven. 2000. *On writing: A memoir of the craft*. London: Hodder and Stoughton.
Kopp, Sheldon B. 1972. *If you meet a buddha on the road, Kill him! The pilgrimage of psychotherapy patients*. New York: Bantam Books.
———. 1973. *Guru: Metaphors from a psychotherapist*. Science and Behavior Books, Inc.
Lamb, Nancy. 2008. *The art and craft of storytelling. A comprehensive guide to classic writing techniques*. Ohio: F + W Media.
Le Guin, Ursula K. 2019. *The carrier bag theory of fiction*. UK: Ignota Books.
Maté, Gabor. 2011. *When the body says no: The cost of hidden stress*. Toronto: Vintage Canada.
May, Rollo. 1975. *The courage to create*. New York: WW Norton & Company.
Mead, Geoff. 2011. *Coming home to story. Storytelling beyond happily ever after*. Bristol: Vala.
———. 2014. *Telling the story: The heart and soul of successful leadership*. West-Sussex: Jossey-Bass.
Mintzberg, Henry. 2017. Developing theory about the development of theory. In *Handbook of middle management strategy process research*, ed. Steven W. Floyd and Bill Wooldridge, 177–196. Northampton: Edward Elgar Publishing.
Neff, Kristin. 2011. *Self Compassion: Stop beating yourself up and leave insecurity behind*. UK: HarperCollins.
Oelrich, Inger Lise. 2015. *The new story: Storytelling as a pathway to peace*. Cornwall: Matador.
Rittel, Horst W.J., and Melvin M. Webber. 1973. Dilemmas in a general theory of planning. *Policy Sciences* 4 (2): 155–169.
Solnit, Rebecca. 2019. When the hero is the problem: On Robert Mueller, Greta Thunberg, and finding strength in numbers. *Literary hub*, April 2. https://lithub.com/rebecca-solnit-when-the-hero-is-the-problem/.

Collaborative Storytelling: A practitioner's guide

TILES: Mosaic of values (Mosaico de valores)

TRADE TROCA	INCLUSION INCLUSÃO	LIBERTY LIBERDADE	EQUILIBRIUM EQUILÍBRIO	SUSTAINABILITY SUSTENTABILIDADE

Our code of conduct is formed by a mosaic of values, referred to as **TILES**. Those values are connected with our story and with how we wish to relate to our community: of clients, collaborators, and partners in practice.
While "trade, inclusion, liberty, equilibrium and sustainability" are the values we promote externally (to potential clients), there are other values we incorporate into our collaborative practices.

O nosso código de conduta é formado por um mosaico de valores (TILES). Tais valores estão conectados à nossa história e a forma que esperamos nos relacionar com a nossa comunidade: de clientes, colaboradores e parceiros.
Apesar dos valores "troca, inclusão, liberdade, e sustentabilidade" serem promovidos externamente (à clientes em potencial), contamos com outros valores em nossas práticas colaborativas.

T	**Trade,** Time, Trust & Transparency	**T**	**Troca**, Tempo, Confiança e Transparência
I	**Inclusion,** Intention & Information	**I**	**Inclusão**, Intenção, Informação
L	**Liberty** and Leadership	**L**	**Liberdade** e Liderança
E	**Equilibrium** (x 8 wellness dimensions)	**E**	**Equilíbrio** (x 8 dimensões do bem-estar)
S	**Sustainable** Stories	**S**	**Sustentabilidade** nas histórias

T. Cleland Silva, P. de Tarso Fonseca Silva, *Making Sense of Work Through Collaborative Storytelling*,
https://doi.org/10.1007/978-3-030-89446-7

(continued)

TRADE (TROCA)	
We value trade in regard to service and learning through mutual partnership, prioritising collaborative work with respect, comradery and empathy.	Valorizamos a troca relacionada à serviços e ao aprendizado através de parcerias mútuas, priorizando o trabalho colaborativo com respeito, camaradagem e empatia.
We believe that everybody has something to share and contribute, to teach or to learn. By actively listening to people's stories, we are able to identify opportunities in our own story (as individuals and as a company), potentially having a positive influence on how we deliver our services and develop our work in the future.	Acreditamos que todos têm algo para compartilhar e contribuir, (ensinando ou aprendendo). Ao exercitar a "escuta ativa", somos capazes de identificar oportunidades em nossa própria história (como indivíduos e como empresa), podendo influenciar positivamente a maneira como oferecemos serviços e desenvolvemos nosso trabalho no futuro.
We trust in our methodology as a tool for **sharing and exchanging** knowledge, using stories as means to communicate, connect, and collaborate.	Confiamos em nossa metodologia como ferramenta de **compartilhamento e troca** de conhecimentos, incorporando histórias como meio de comunicação, conexão e colaboração.
TIME (TEMPO)	
Time is a valuable resource to all and we put a conscious effort to use it wisely.	**Tempo** é um recurso valioso para todos e nossa intenção é utilizar esse recurso de forma consciente.
Time is used to frame our client's stories as well as our priorities within Metaphora International's work.	O **tempo** é usado para estruturar as histórias de nossos clientes e as prioridades do nosso trabalho como Metaphora International.
The very nature of "story craft" requires a "**timeline**" and the same applies to our mindset on developing projects, structured around our lifestyle.	Em sua essência, o processo de "story craft" utiliza uma "**linha do tempo**" e o mesmo também se aplica ao desenvolvimento de projetos estruturados para acomodar o nosso estilo de vida.
The value of time should be acknowledged holistically, taking into account our choices and values as individuals, but also with our social responsibilities and interests, beyond work.	**O valor do tempo deve ser conceituado** de forma holística, considerando nossos valores e escolhas como indivíduos, com interesses e responsabilidades além do trabalho.
As a family-oriented business, we expect to keep a healthy balance with collaborative work. By applying the value TRADE, we also welcome flexibility, and aim to be empathetic to the time of our collaborators.	Como uma empresa familiar, esperamos manter um equilíbrio saudável com trabalho colaborativo. Ao exercitar o valor TROCA, também vinculamos flexibilidade e empatia ao tempo dos nossos colaboradores.
We hope to rely on commitments through accountability and transparent communication.	Esperamos poder contar com a responsabilidade e o comprometimento mútuos, através de uma comunicação transparente.

(*continued*)

(continued)

TRUST & TRANSPARENCY (CONFIANÇA e TRANSPARÊNCIA)	
Trust is directly related with liability, **transparency,** and active communication between both parties.	A **confiança** está diretamente relacionada à responsabilidade, **transparência** e comunicação ativa entre ambas as partes.
Trust relates to everything we do together. Every activity associated with our brand is represented by or associated with people that we **trust**.	A **confiança** influencia tudo que fazemos juntos. Toda atividade associada à nossa marca é representada ou associada a pessoas em quem confiamos.
For **trust** to continue to be nurtured in our collaborative story, we expect **transparency** and an open dialogue on	Para que a confiança continue sendo nutrida em nossa história de colaboração, esperamos **transparência** e um diálogo aberto sobre
(1) The on-going level of motivation in the collaboration: purpose with authenticity should remain clear, to ensure that time and talent are not wasted in both parties.	(1) O nível de motivação na colaboração corrente: propósito com autenticidade devem permanecer claros para que tempo e talento em ambas as partes não sejam desperdiçados.
(2) How eventual changes should be incorporated into our agreements and the commitments (towards our work and our community).	(2) Como eventuais mudanças devem ser incorporadas nos acordos e compromissos do nosso trabalho em relação à nossa comunidade.
(3) Consensus on the use of our tools and our brand, where parallel activities performed (independently) by collaborators should respect our privacy and intellectual property without conflicting with our consulting business as storytelling practitioners.	(3) Consenso no uso de nossas ferramentas e nossa marca, sabendo que atividades paralelas executadas (independentemente) por colaboradores devem respeitar nossa privacidade e propriedade intelectual sem entrar em conflito com nossas práticas de consultoria associadas ao "storytelling" e às narrativas.
INCLUSION (INCLUSÃO)	
INCLUSION represents a mindset of being aware of differences with a respectful attitude towards the "journey" of others. We believe that differences are also learning opportunities for our growth (personal and as a business).	A **INCLUSÃO** representa uma mentalidade de reconhecer diferenças com uma atitude respeitosa à "jornada" dos outros. Acreditamos que diferenças também são oportunidades de aprendizado para nosso crescimento (pessoal e como negócio).
In the context of Metaphora International, **inclusion** does not mean incorporating every and any personal value into our practices. Instead, it promotes curiosity and the willingness to establish a "compromising zone" for collaboration which is aligned with the profile of our community and which does not contradict our values as a whole (TILES).	No contexto da Metaphora International, **inclusão** não significa incorporar todo e qualquer valor pessoal em nossas práticas. Mas ser curioso e disposto em estabelecer uma "zona de comprometimento" para a colaboração, que seja alinhada ao perfil de nossa comunidade, sem contradizer nossos valores como um todo (TILES).

(continued)

(continued)

With our clients, **inclusion** represents a genuine interest in their world view allowing us to work with their stories without pre-judgment. We aim to be receptive to their needs by putting a conscious effort to incorporate their wishes into our services, as much as possible.	Com nossos clientes, a **inclusão** representa o interesse genuíno em sua visão de mundo, trabalhando com suas histórias sem pré-julgamento. Nosso objetivo é ser receptivo às suas necessidades, com a intenção consciente de acomodar em nossos serviços suas preferências, dentro de nossas possibilidades.
INTENTION (INTENÇÃO)	
INTENTION relates to how engaged we are with our purpose as individuals and our goals as a business.	**INTENÇÃO** refere-se a quão engajados estamos com nosso propósito (como indivíduos e nossos objetivos como empresa).
It means to consciously apply our talents to good use: to communicate our visions and needs respectfully and share the responsibility of maintaining a friendly atmosphere with the members of our community.	Significa aplicar conscientemente nossos talentos: comunicar respeitosamente nossas visões e necessidades e compartilhar a responsabilidade de manter uma atmosfera amigável com os membros de nossa comunidade.
As a consulting business working with narrative, intention also means that we make sense of the stories we work with by framing our operations as "activities" (in reference to Activity Theory). As such, we are expected to identify the objective, motivation, or intention of each service or project as early as possible.	Como empresa de consultoria que trabalha com narrativas, a **intenção** também significa interesse em interpretar as histórias com as quais trabalhamos como "atividades" (em referência à Teoria da Atividade). Desta forma, a **intenção** é identificar o objetivo ou motivação de cada serviço ou projeto, o mais cedo possível.
Identifying the **intention** behind each activity (from our clients and community) also supports us in organising our time and how we **intend** to collaborate, plan, commit, and accomplish our goals.	Identificar a intenção por trás de cada atividade (de nossos clientes e de nossa comunidade) também nos ajuda a organizar nosso tempo e como pretendemos colaborar e planejar nossas ações para atingir nossos objetivos.
INFORMATION (INFORMAÇÃO)	
INFORMATION is power. Metaphora International has strong roots in academia and creates methods based on scientific research and personal stories. And yet, our methods are pragmatic and have the intention to help support our community in real life situations.	**INFORMAÇÃO é poder.** A Metaphora International tem fortes raízes na academia e cria métodos baseados em pesquisas científicas. No entanto, nossos métodos são pragmáticos e têm a intenção de ajudar a apoiar nossa comunidade em situações da vida real.

(*continued*)

(continued)

Making **information** available must be a priority and an intention in all levels of collaboration. This applies to everyone who sees himself/herself as a member of the Metaphora International close community. As soon as someone identifies the lack of **information** on a particular topic or activity, the same individual should factor in his/her position as collaborator to contribute to resolve the issue with resourceful **information or questions**. We would like to have the resources to make **informed decisions.**	A disponibilização de **informações** deve ser uma prioridade e uma intenção em todos os níveis de colaboração. Isso se aplica a todos que se consideram membros da comunidade de colaboradores da Metaphora International. Assim que alguém identificar a falta de **informações** sobre um tópico ou atividade, o mesmo indivíduo deve levar em consideração sua posição como colaborador e sua contribuição para resolver o problema com **informações** úteis ou perguntas.
Internally, we encourage **information** to be categorised by themes to facilitate collaborative practices and help us to organise the order of priorities with time and other commitments.	Internamente, sugerimos que as **informações** sejam categorizadas por temas, a fim de facilitar práticas colaborativas e nos ajudar a organizar a ordem de prioridades, considerando tempo e outros compromissos.
LIBERTY & LEADERSHIP (LIBERDADE e LIDERANÇA)	
LIBERTY refers to the freedom of the collaborative parties to gauge and decide how well the collaboration is aligned with their own expectations. Everyone is trusted to **lead** their own story and apply their own talents in accordance with their purpose—as long as it does not conflict with our code of conduct.	A **LIBERDADE** refere-se à possibilidade de avaliar e decidir o quanto essa colaboração está alinhada com suas próprias expectativas. Confiamos que todos têm o poder de **liderar** sua própria história e aplicar seus próprios talentos de acordo com seu propósito—contanto que suas ações não entrem em conflito com nosso código de conduta.
Within Metaphora International, when a collaborator is appointed to **lead** a project, he or she is expected to take initiative while being transparent and informative, by including the co-founders in the decisions that are associated with our brand. In other words, in line with our mosaic of values as a whole (TILES), everyone has the **liberty** to define the level of commitment invested from the beginning of the collaboration or to end the collaboration indefinitely, after agreements related to collaborative projects have been fulfilled.	Quando um colaborador é nomeado para **liderar** um projeto, esperamos que ele/ela tome iniciativa quanto ao que deve ser feito, mantendo as informações transparentes e incluindo os co-fundadores nas decisões associadas à Metaphora International. Em outras palavras, de acordo com nosso mosaico de valores como um todo (TILES), todos têm a **liberdade** de definir o nível de comprometimento investido em nosso trabalho no início da colaboração ou de finalizar a colaboração indefinidamente, após tratados referentes a projetos colaborativos tenham sido concluídos.

(continued)

(continued)

With clients, **liberty** means to remind them that all of us are free to craft, tell, and pursue our own story. The same freedom is promoted with our collaborators as a way to apply their **self-leadership** skills within our community.	Com os clientes, **liberdade** significa lembrá-los de que todos nós somos livres para criar, contar e seguir nossa própria história. A mesma **liberdade** é promovida a nossos colaboradores ao aplicarem suas habilidades de **auto-liderança** em nossa comunidade.
EQUILIBRIUM (EQUILÍBRIO)	
The work with Metaphora International originated to pursue everything we are inspired to do around storytelling as a human activity. On a personal level, working with Collaborative Story Craft has considered a holistic approach to our vocation, as an extension of our lifestyle.	O trabalho com a Metaphora International originou-se como uma maneira de desenvolver e aplicar tudo que nos inspira em torno do processo de criar e contar histórias como atividade humana. Em um nível pessoal, trabalhar com o Collaborative Story Craft considerou uma visão holística da nossa vocação, como extensão do nosso estilo de vida.
To maintain a healthy balance between personal and professional time, we pay attention to the variables that complement our own story. In this process, we aim to understand all dimensions of well-being and how we should prioritise them in line with our purpose.	Para manter um equilíbrio saudável entre tempo pessoal e profissional, prestamos atenção nas variáveis que complementam nossa história. Nesse processo, buscamos entender todas as dimensões do bem-estar e como deveríamos priorizá-las em relação ao nosso propósito.
Knowing how we prioritise each of our wellness dimensions (**physical, emotional, environmental, intellectual, occupational, financial, social, and spiritual**), allows us not only to plan our work better but also to act on improving our well-being as a whole.	Saber como priorizamos cada uma das dimensões do bem-estar (**físico, emocional, ambiental, intelectual, ocupacional, financeiro, social e espiritual**), permite não só planejar melhor o nosso trabalho, mas também agir para melhorar nosso bem-estar como um todo.
SUSTAINABILITY (SUSTENTABILIDADE)	
We believe that the choices that we make impact not only our story but also a bigger story: with our social dynamics and the environment we live in.	Acreditamos que as escolhas que fazemos impactam, não apenas a nossa história, mas também uma história maior: com nossa dinâmica social e o ambiente em que vivemos.
Sustainability in our work means to take responsibility for how our story and our practices are connected with our intentions and decisions.	**Sustentabilidade** em nosso trabalho significa assumir a responsabilidade de como nossa história e nossas práticas estão conectadas com nossas intenções e decisões.

(*continued*)

(continued)

Before starting any collaborative project, the parties must ensure that there is no risk of unethical activities to be linked with our work and that whatever contribution we make, it should be aligned and/or complementary to our values (TILES). Valuing sustainability and incorporating it to Collaborative Storytelling work represents a conscious effort on nurturing long lasting stories of purpose for the common good: starting with our collaboration and extending to the projects we are involved with.	Antes de iniciar qualquer projeto colaborativo, os colaboradores devem se certificar que não há o risco de atividades antiéticas estarem vinculadas ao nosso trabalho e que qualquer contribuição de nossa parte deve ser alinhada e/ou complementar os nossos valores (TILES). Valorizar a **sustentabilidade** incorporada ao trabalho com Collaborative Storytelling representa um esforço consciente em nutrir histórias com propósito duradouro para o bem comum: começando com a nossa colaboração e estendendo-se aos projetos em que estamos envolvidos.

Collaborative Story Craft as a Tool (Collaborative Story Craft como ferramenta)

Collaborative Story Craft is a working tool developed by the co-founders of Metaphora International. The tool enables the materialisation of stories and learning exchange alongside collaborators. *Collaborative Story Craft* incorporates several fields of knowledge (practical, theoretical, and philosophical), that enable the conceptualisation of individual and collective identity, sensemaking of purpose through the analysis of narratives and by using storytelling techniques for individual and organisational work. As an umbrella concept, *Collaborative Story Craft* is in fact a set of tools, and it embodies different terminologies that complement the method, such as: ***Story Mediation,Nurturing the Roots,Metaphorical Tourism and Mentorship Mosaic.***	Nosso método *Collaborative Story Craft* é uma ferramenta de trabalho desenvolvida pelos co-fundadores da Metaphora International. A ferramenta possibilita a materialização de histórias e a troca de experiências junto aos colaboradores. O *Collaborative Story Craft* incorpora diversos campos do conhecimento (prático, teórico e filosófico), permitindo a conceituação de identidade (individual ou coletiva) e a análise de propósito através de histórias, utilizando técnicas narrativas para o trabalho pessoal e organizacional. Com uma perspectiva abrangente, o *Collaborative Story Craft* é um conjunto de ferramentas e incorpora diferentes terminologias que complementam o método. Alguns exemplos incluem: ***Mediação de Histórias, Nutrindo as Raízes, Turismo Metafórico e Mosaico de Mentores.***

(*continued*)

Story Mediation (Mediação de Histórias)

Story mediation is the process of enabling others to express their own stories (in different formats). It aims to capture authenticity by analysing and documenting themes and metaphors, and it involves a conscious effort to empower rather than influence the story.	A *mediação de histórias* é o processo de capacitar outras pessoas a expressar suas próprias histórias (em diferentes formatos). O objetivo da *mediação de histórias* é capturar autenticidade através da análise e documentação de temas e metáforas, e envolve um esforço consciente para capacitar e não influenciar a história.
Story mediation is connected with the method of *Collaborative Story Craft*, which requires preparation with a team of qualified *Story Mediators*. In order for the *story mediation* to take place, it is necessary to provide a safe environment, allowing the storyteller to express his/her own views without feeling judged by external values.	A *mediação de histórias* está conectada com o método do *Collaborative Story Craft*, que por sua vez precisa de uma equipe de mediadores de histórias qualificados. Para que a mediação da história ocorra, é necessário fornecer um ambiente seguro, permitindo que o narrador expresse suas próprias opiniões sem se sentir julgado por valores externos.

Our mission is to empower authentic stories
and help people work better together.
Nossa missão é capacitar histórias autênticas
e ajudar pessoas a trabalharem melhor juntas.

Index[1]

[1] Note: Page numbers followed by 'n' refer to notes.

T. Cleland Silva, P. de Tarso Fonseca Silva, *Making Sense of Work Through Collaborative Storytelling*,
https://doi.org/10.1007/978-3-030-89446-7

The manufacturer's authorised representative in the EU is Springer Nature Customer Service Centre GmbH, Europaplatz 3, 69115 Heidelberg, Germany. If you have any concerns regarding our products, please contact ProductSafety@springernature.com

Printed and bound by CPI Group (UK) Ltd, Croydon, CR0 4YY
30/09/2026
02225514-0007